Executive Summary

The purpose of this report is to shed light on the poorly understood role that Yunus Khalis played in modern Afghan political history. This research is based on an analysis of several under-studied primary sources in Pashto and Persian that offer unique insight into Khalis's life and work. Although he was an author, teacher and the leader of the Hizb-e Islami (Khalis) mujahidin political party during the Soviet Afghan War, today Yunus Khalis is most often discussed in the context of his personal relationships with Jalaluddin Haqqani and Usama bin Ladin. There is little doubt that Khalis was on friendly terms with these two men. However, Haqqani had a far more visible effect on the growth of al-Qa`ida than Khalis, and the latter apparently had major political disagreements with Bin Ladin. This report will argue that Yunus Khalis's historical impact is better found in his work as an activist intellectual and his refusal to take sides in the Afghan Civil War than in his relatively peripheral contact with Usama bin Ladin.

According to the available sources, Yunus Khalis did not play a major role in the Haqqani Network's diversification as a financial, criminal and terrorist enterprise, and he also had little direct role in al-Qa`ida's growth after the Battle of Zhawara. Even so, the Khalis biographies fill some of the gaps in other sources about Bin Ladin's arrival in Nangarhar in 1996. This helps pinpoint with increasing confidence the identity of the Afghan mujahidin commanders who were most closely involved in the return of the al-Qa`ida leadership to Afghanistan. Additionally, these biographies offer hitherto unknown details about the history of Khalis's base at Tora Bora and the critical role that Haqqani played in helping Khalis to begin an organized fight against the Soviets.

Since so little is known about Yunus Khalis's life and career, the first section of this report will draw together the most important available details of his biography. This will provide the proper context for the discussion of Khalis's contact with Bin Ladin, Haqqani and Mullah Omar in the second section. The main details from these two sections and the implications associated with this report are briefly summarized below.

Yunus Khalis's Life and Career up to the Soviet-Afghan War

- Yunus Khalis was a prolific writer in Pashto and Persian who published dozens of books and articles, and edited and wrote for several journals and magazines during the 1950s and 1970s. Most of his work was on religious and political themes, and included translations of books by Sayyid Qutb, Ibn Taymiyya and Gustave Le Bon.

- Khalis was more closely involved with the frontline fighting during the Soviet Afghan War than any other Afghan leader of equivalent rank. He apparently took a small group of fighters with him to begin resisting the Soviets in Nangarhar before he had even formed his political party. Instead of providing weapons to the men who would eventually become his commanders, Khalis was initially dependent upon supplies he received from Jalaluddin Haqqani and Mati'ullah Khan.

- Khalis's political party was first formed when Jalaluddin Haqqani, Mati'ullah Khan and (possibly) Jamil al-Rahman agreed to begin fighting together and form a party called Hizb-e Islami under Yunus Khalis's leadership.

- The Tora Bora base in Pachir aw Agam District was the third Nangarhari base occupied by Hizb-e Islami (Khalis) in the late 1970s, and it became one of the party's most important regional hubs. In spite of later events, there is no evidence that Tora Bora played a significant role in the early development of al-Qa`ida in the late 1980s.

Yunus Khalis's Personal Ties to Bin Ladin, al-Qa`ida and Mullah Omar

- Nangarhar Province was not free from the factional violence that eventually led to the Afghan Civil War from 1992 to 1996, but the province was able to avoid the worst ravages of that violence under the leadership of the Eastern Shura in Jalalabad, potentially as a result of direction that Khalis provided.

- When Khalis returned to Afghanistan from Peshawar, Pakistan, in the mid-1990s, he created a new housing development on the south side of Jalalabad. This development was initially called Najm al-Jihad in reference to its proximity to the tomb of the famed Mullah of Hadda, Najm al-Din Akhundzada. This large neighborhood is now variously known as "Khalis Families" and "Khalis Colony," and it was here that Khalis hosted Bin Ladin for a brief period during 1996.

- When Bin Ladin was exiled from Sudan in early 1996, he gave Khalis so much credit for his willingness to help host al-Qa`ida's leadership that he called Khalis "the Father Sheikh." Noteworthy as this may be, many of Khalis's followers referred to him in a similar fashion as a sign of respect, and there is no available evidence that Khalis ever acted as a mentor to Usama bin Ladin.

- Three important Nangarhar-based commanders were apparently instrumental in bringing Usama bin Ladin to Jalalabad when he was exiled from Sudan in 1996. These men were Engineer Mahmud of Hizb-e Islami (Khalis), Haji Saz Nur of the Ittihad-e Islami party, and Fazl al-Haq Mujahid of Hizb-e Islami (Gulbuddin). Although their assistance was briefly essential to the al-Qa`ida leader's return to Afghanistan, it is helpful to remember that Haqqani maintained a close operational relationship with al-Qa`ida camps in Paktia and Khost throughout the 1990s.

- Available evidence suggests that Bin Ladin agreed to go to Jalalabad when he was exiled from Sudan in a large part because the area controlled by his closest ally in Afghanistan, Jalaluddin Haqqani, was already under Taliban command. Nangarhar was still free from the Taliban in early 1996, and Bin Ladin's decision to go there appears to have been made in part because he did not yet trust the Taliban.

- Khalis was initially favorable to the Taliban, and he advised Jalaluddin Haqqani not to fight when their forces arrived in Paktia. However, Khalis disagreed with many of the Taliban's more extreme policies, and his attempts to negotiate a settlement between the Taliban and the Northern Alliance after 1996 were ignored. There is little information about Khalis's interactions with Mullah Omar, but the scant available evidence indicates that these two were neither friends nor political allies.

- Various sources attest that Yunus Khalis strongly disagreed with Bin Ladin's plan to declare a jihad against the Saudi Kingdom and the American forces stationed there in 1996. One source even relates that Khalis tried to broker negotiations between Bin Ladin and the Saudi government, but these talks apparently fell through because of the unacceptable preconditions that Bin Ladin set for a normalization of relations.

Implications

Contrary to the commonly held view that al-Qa`ida has been based exclusively in the most unstable and weakly governed areas, Usama bin Ladin and his lieutenants returned to Nangarhar in 1996 primarily because the area around Jalalabad was both calm and under the control of a relatively strong political body that was mostly uninterested in al-Qa`ida's operational agenda. This raises uncomfortable questions about the minimum conditions required for a terrorist organization like al-Qa`ida to maintain a presence in Afghanistan. Nangarhar offered Usama bin Ladin an attractive combination of relative peace, active support from friendly regional leaders like Engineer Mahmud and Haji Saz Nur, and a local governing body in the Eastern Shura that was more focused on maintaining security and trade in the province than harassing extremist groups like al-Qa'ida.

If that combination of a limited but loyal local support network and lack of interference from nearby governing bodies is any indication of what it takes for a major terrorist organization to find a safe haven in Afghanistan, then it may be wise to take pronouncements of the imminent destruction of al-Qa'ida or affiliated organizations with a grain of salt. Leaving aside the question of the current operational capacity of al-Qa'ida, the findings in this report serve as a warning to any who suppose that a moderate level of security and government presence is sufficient to prevent al-Qa'ida or a similar organization from maintaining safe havens in Afghanistan.

Although elements of the Taliban are now more openly hostile to al-Qa'ida, the Afghan central government is unable to project a strong security and governance presence in all of the districts in eastern Afghanistan. In places like Giro District of Ghazni Province, the current local government has essentially no capacity to influence what happens outside the walls of the district compound. In that kind of permissive environment, all al-Qa'ida might need to survive in the area is a reliable local partner.

It may not be possible for al-Qa'ida to thrive in Afghanistan as it did in the days before 9/11, but the threshold required for the organization's continued existence may be lower than is commonly suspected. Clearly, the international community must continue to focus on eroding the diminishing military and operational capabilities of al-Qa'ida and similar movements. However, the primary sources about Yunus Khalis's life remind us that even when al-Qa'ida's leadership was managing a period of significant transition, Usama bin Ladin's organization was able to survive locally with little more than help from a few friends in Nangarhar and Loya Paktia, and a distracted or disinterested local governing body in Jalalabad.

Map of Nangarhar Province and the Surrounding Area

Contents

Introduction

The year 1996 was a watershed moment for Usama bin Ladin. It was a time of transition in which he fled Sudan in exile, returned to Afghanistan with the leadership of al-Qaʿida and wrote a letter (*risala*) declaring war against the Saudi Kingdom and the United States. Prior to publishing his risala in August of that year,[1] Usama bin Ladin sought legal backing for a declaration of jihad against the ongoing American presence in Saudi Arabia from prominent religious scholars (*ʿulama*) including Yunus Khalis.[2] The scant available evidence suggests that at that time Bin Ladin and Khalis had a friendly relationship dating back to the days of the anti-Soviet jihad, when Yunus Khalis had led one of the most important mujahidin political parties in eastern Afghanistan.[3] In fact, Bin Ladin was probably staying in a residence at Khalis's Najm al-

---

[1] Usama bin Ladin. "Bin Laden's Fatwa." *PBS News Hour,* as printed in *al-Quds al-ʾArabi*, 23 August 1996. www.pbs.org/newshour/updates/military/july-dec96/fatwa_1996.html. Bin Ladin's *risala* is often referred to as a *fatwa* (a legal opinion based on Islamic law), but this is probably incorrect. Bin Ladin does not appear to have used this term, and it is misleading to think of the document as a legal opinion.

[2] Haji Din Muhammad. *The Life, Art, and Thought of Mawlawi Khalis.* (Hayatabad, Peshawar: Pir Chap Khuna, 2007), 203. Bin Ladin apparently also discussed the need to expel the Americans from Saudi Arabia with Mullah Omar at some point in 1996 and was rebuffed. This conversation seems to have taken place after Bin Ladin published his risala. See Alex Linschoten and Felix Kuehn. *An Enemy We Created: the Myth of the Taliban/al-Qaeda Merger in Afghanistan, 1970-2010.* (London: Oxford University Press, 2012), 140.

[3] The best evidence for a close friendship between Bin Ladin and Yunus Khalis comes from ʿAbd al-Kabir Talai's biography of Khalis and a memoir written by Usama bin Ladin's son Omar. See 'Abd al-Kabir Talai. *Khalis Baba Step by Step.* (Peshawar: Ihsan Publishing Society, 2012), 93–97; and Omar bin Laden, Najwa bin Laden, and Jean Sasson. *Growing Up bin Ladin: Osama's Wife and Son Take Us Inside Their Secret World.* (New York: St. Martin's Press, 2009), 154–155. To date, ʿAbd al-Kabir Talai is the only known primary source who goes so far as to state that Bin Ladin viewed Khalis as a father figure. Talai relates that the al-Qaʿida leader spoke reverently of Khalis as "al-Sheikh al-Walid" (the Father Sheikh) because Khalis supported Bin Ladin when the rest of the world was turning against him. See Talai, 96. Mary Anne Weaver also has something to say about the relationship between the two men, even if it seems somewhat conjectural: "'Khalis had an avuncular interest in bin Laden,' Michael Scheuer, the former head of the C.I.A.'s bin Ladin unit and the author of 'Imperial Hubris,' told me recently when we met at a Washington coffeehouse. 'Osama lost his father when he was young, and Khalis became a substitute father figure to him. As far as Khalis was concerned, he considered Osama the perfect Islamic youth.'" See Mary Anne Weaver. "Lost at Tora Bora." (*New York Times.* 2005 11-September), www.nytimes.com/2005/09/11/magazine/11TORABORA.html?pagewanted=all&_r=0; and Jeffrey Dressler and Reza Jan. "The Haqqani Network in Kurram: The Regional Implications of a Growing Insurgency." (Washington, D.C.: The Institute for the Study of War, 2011), 4. Jere Van Dyk also comments on the relationship between Bin Ladin and Khalis. See especially Jere Van Dyk. "My Friend the Afghan Warlord." (*The Baltimore Sun.* 2006 28-September). http://articles.baltimoresun.com/2006-09-28/news/0609280013_1_afghanistan-mujahedeen-god.

Jihad neighborhood shortly before he issued a call for support for his forthcoming declaration of jihad.[4] But if Bin Ladin was hoping for a positive response on the basis of his personal connection to Khalis, he was to be disappointed.[5]

In his answer to Usama bin Ladin, Khalis reasoned that as long as the lawful government in Riyadh continued to allow the Americans to stay as guests, then no jihad was permissible.[6] Additionally, Khalis argued that it was foolish to work for the overthrow of the Saudi government since any replacement would probably be a less enthusiastic supporter of Islamic law (*shari'a*).[7] In other words, Khalis apparently rebuked Usama bin Ladin's extremist ideology at the precise moment when the al-Qa'ida leader had chosen to publicly declare an international jihad against the Saudi Kingdom and its American allies.

'Abd al-Kabir Talai[8] expands on this anecdote by explaining that Yunus Khalis had initially attempted to mediate between the Saudi government and Usama bin Ladin after the relationship between the two parties soured earlier in the 1990s.[9] According to Talai's account, Khalis was able to get the Saudis to agree to negotiate with Bin Ladin, but the talks fell through because the al-Qa'ida leader set unacceptable conditions for a normalization of relations.[10] Even though Bin Ladin apparently appreciated Khalis's friendship and personal support enough to refer to him as "the Father Sheikh,"[11] the

---

[4] Elsewhere in Din Muhammad's biography of Khalis, this neighborhood is known as Najm al-Jihad, but in this particular citation, he writes that "and he [Bin Ladin] lived for some time in Jalalabad city, and then he took up residence in a house at the 'families' of Mawlawi Khalis." See Muhammad (2007), 202. This is essentially the same place as Najm al-Jihad, and in fact, closely matches the "Khalis Families" name provided for the neighborhood on UN maps and the Jalalabad area map on Google Earth.

[5] Ibid., 203–204. Din Muhammad paraphrases Khalis's response to Osama bin Ladin.

[6] Ibid., 204.

[7] Ibid., 203. More specifically, Khalis remarks that the Saudi government enforces the sanctioned punishments (*hudud*), collects the alms tax (*zakat*), prays properly, commands right and forbids wrong (*amr bi 'l-ma'ruf wa 'n-nahy 'an al-munkar*) etc.

[8] Talai is one of Khalis's biographers, but otherwise little is known about him. Unlike Ahmadzai, Talai is not shy about discussing Khalis's connections to Bin Ladin.

[9] Talai, 95–96.

[10] Ibid., 95–96. As it is elsewhere confirmed, Bin Ladin demanded that the American forces in Saudi Arabia be replaced with al-Qa'ida mujahidin. Talai does not state when Khalis arranged these negotiations between the Saudis and Bin Ladin, but it must have been well before Bin Ladin published his risala in 1996.

[11] Ibid., 96.

only known primary sources relate that every time Khalis offered Bin Ladin political advice, the al-Qa`ida leader ignored him.[12]

These episodes, never before reported in the secondary literature, come from a group of several previously unstudied primary sources in Pashto on the life of Yunus Khalis, which form the basis of this report.[13] These sources are an excellent starting point for a critique of the current literature on Khalis's connection to al-Qa`ida, in part because they depart so radically from the currently dominant depictions of Yunus Khalis as an ultraconservative sexual predator[14] who became the key al-Qa`ida supporter in Nangarhar when Bin Ladin fled Sudan.[15]

---

[12] The two known instances are Khalis's response to Bin Ladin's call for support for his forthcoming declaration of jihad in 1996, and Khalis's attempts to get Bin Ladin to compromise with the Saudi government. See Muhammad (2007), 202–204; and Talai, 95–96.

[13] In addition to the aforementioned biographies of Khalis written by Haji Din Muhammad and 'Abd al-Kabir Talai, this report makes use of a group of new sources in Pashto and Persian. See especially Puhnamal Zahidi Ahmadzai. *Khalis Baba upon the Road of Eternity*. (Peshawar: Amir Kruwr Kitabtun, 2006); Muhammad Yunus Khalis. *The Islamic World Today and Yesterday*. Edited by 'Abdul Hadi Mullah Khel. (Peshawar: Ihsan Khparanduya Tulana, 2002). This last book is a collection of Khalis's essays from the *Gahiz* journal. For reasons of linguistic clarity, sometimes reference is made to the 2008 Persian translation of Din Muhammad's biography of Khalis. See Haji Din Muhammad. *The Life, Art, and Thought of Mawlawi Khalis*. Translated by Majib al-Rahman Amiri. (Kabul: Samim Khparanduya Tulana, 2008). Some additional information can be gathered from the brief biographical entry on Khalis written by Shohrat Nangyal. See Shohrat Nangyal. *Blood on the Pen*. (Peshawar: De Afghanistan de Jihadi Tsirrunu Markaz, 1989). As of writing, I have only analyzed the portion of Talai's biography that bears directly on Khalis's relationship with Usama bin Ladin. See Talai, 93–97.

[14] For typical examples of authors' discussing Khalis's alleged sexual interest in teenage girls, see Lawrence Wright. *The Looming Tower: al Qaeda and the Road to 9/11*. (New York: Vintage Books, 2007), 255; Steve Coll. *Ghost Wars: the Secret History of the CIA, Afghanistan, and bin Ladin, from the Soviet Invasion to September 10, 2001*. (New York: Penguin Books, 2004), 327; Van Dyk (2006); and Peter Tomsen. *The Wars of Afghanistan: Messianic Terrorism, Tribal Conflicts, and the Failures of Great Powers*. (New York: Public Affairs, 2011), 303.

[15] For authors who discuss Khalis as Bin Ladin's host in 1996, see Peter Bergen. *The Osama bin Laden I Know*. (New York: Free Press, 2006), 159; Michael Scheuer. *Through Our Enemies' Eyes: Osama bin Laden, Radical Islam, and the Future of America*. 2nd. (Dulles: Potomac Books, Inc., 2006), 164–165; Michael Scheuer. *Osama Bin Laden*. (New York: Oxford University Press, 2011), 105–106; Tomsen, 543, 608; Barnett Rubin *The Fragmentation of Afghanistan: State Formation and Collapse in the International System*. 2nd. (New Haven: Yale University Press, 2002), xxvii; Wright, 255; Coll, 327; Weaver (2005); and also Gretchen Peters. *How Opium Profits the Taliban*. (Washington, D.C.: U.S. Institute of Peace, 2009), 8. For authors who mention Bin Ladin's connections to Khalis's old base at Tora Bora in Nangarhar, see Scheuer (2011), 106, 131; Tomsen, 250, 608; Wright, 259–260; and Weaver (2005). For authors who mention Khalis helping Usama bin Ladin to escape from U.S. forces in 2001, see Tomsen, 608; Weaver (2005). Van Dyk and Smucker claim that Khalis's son helped Bin Ladin escape. See Van Dyk (2006); and Smucker, Phillip. "On the Case in Tora Bora." (*Asia Times: South Asia*. 2009 10-April).

Scholars should exercise caution in accepting the entirety of the newly available biographical accounts of Yunus Khalis's life and politics, in part because such accounts have been written by sources who are highly favorable to him. To control for some of this possible bias, it is necessary to compare the relevant portions of the biographies with the other available primary sources about al-Qa'ida and the Afghan mujahidin. The results of such an analysis are surprising and underline how little is known about the ideology and relationships that helped fuel the growth of al-Qa'ida and the Haqqani network. Most important of all, the current sources provide no evidence for the assertion that Yunus Khalis was ever the key operational facilitator for al-Qa'ida in Nangarhar or anywhere else.

If authors such as Michael Scheuer,[16] Mary Anne Weaver[17] and Thomas Lynch[18] are correct in their assessment that the relationship between Usama bin Ladin and Yunus Khalis was critical to al-Qa'ida's supposed transition to Afghanistan in 1996,[19] then one could expect an investigation of this period of Khalis's life to underline the importance of his enthusiasm for al-Qa'ida. But according to the biographies considered here, Khalis's material support for al-Qa'ida was an extension of his personal relationship with Bin Ladin and remained limited to providing the al-Qa'ida leader with a place to stay for a short time in 1996.[20] Beyond this act as a host there is no evidence that Khalis facilitated al-Qa'ida operationally. On the other hand, there are various sources indicating that Khalis disagreed with the organization's politics. While his biographers may have political reasons for suppressing this connection, various sources linked to al-

---

www.atimes.com/atimes/South_Asia/KD10Df01.html. Several authors also argue that Khalis introduced Usama bin Ladin to Mullah Omar, although as we will see later, this is unlikely. See Weaver (2005); Dressler and Jan, 4; and Van Dyk (2006).

[16] See especially Scheuer (2011), 105–106.

[17] Weaver (2005).

[18] Thomas Lynch. *The 80 Percent Solution: the Strategic Defeat of bin Laden's al-Qaeda and Implications for South Asian Security.* (New America Foundation, 2012), 23. See the footnote cited on page 23, in which Lynch discusses Khalis's relationship with Bin Ladin.

[19] In truth, al-Qa'ida never left Afghanistan. They maintained bases near Zhawara in Khost throughout the period when the central al-Qa'ida leadership was living in Sudan. See Vahid Brown and Don Rassler. *Manuscript Copy of Fountainhead of Jihad: The Haqqani Nexus, 1973-2010.* (2012). Any discussion of a "return to Afghanistan" must be confined to al-Qa'ida leaders such as Bin Ladin and not the to the organization as a whole.

[20] Ahmadzai is silent about Khalis's possible connection to Bin Ladin, but the other biographers are unequivocal. See Muhammad (2007), 202–204; and Talai, 93-97.

Qa`ida, which are less likely to have any such qualms, tell essentially the same story. Together these accounts suggest that support from provincial-level commanders such as Jalaluddin Haqqani, Haji Saz Nur, Engineer Mahmud and Fazl al-Haq Mujahid had a much more tangible effect on Usama bin Ladin's operations leading up to 1996 than that of the aging Khalis.[21]

The new Pashto material on Khalis helps to add precision to the discussion of Bin Ladin's flight from Sudan to Afghanistan in 1996, but it also emphasizes Khalis's importance as a writer and historical figure before the Soviet-Afghan War. The biographies are often amusing and readily confirm what Peter Tomsen has called Khalis's "famous sense of humor."[22] This material also clearly shows that Khalis must be included amongst the most significant political and intellectual figures of 20th century Afghanistan. He published dozens of articles and books in poetry and prose,[23] was involved in some of the earliest Afghan journalistic publications,[24] and hosted a

---

[21] See Sheikh Muhammad, interview by Anand Gopal. *Unpublished Anand Gopal Interview with Sheikh Muhammad Omar 'Abd al-Rahman* (2012). Sheikh Muhammad Umar 'Abd al-Rahman is the son of "The Blind Sheikh" and was supposedly with Usama bin Ladin when he arrived in Jalalabad in 1996. Din Muhammad also discusses Bin Ladin's coming to Nangarhar; see Muhammad (2007), 202–204. For more information about Jalaluddin Haqqani's prominent role in the growth of al-Qa`ida, see Brown and Rassler (2012). For more on the available al-Qa`ida-connected sources, see Bergen; Scheuer (2011); and Omar bin Laden; and Abu Jandal, Nasir al-Bahri, interview by Khalid al-Hamadi. *An Insider's View of Al-Qa`ida as Narrated by Nasir al-Bahri (Abu Jandal)* (al-Quds al-'Arabi. 2005 23-March).

[22] Peter Tomsen, who met Khalis on a number of occasions, reports that Khalis's humor "occasionally lightened the atmosphere of our otherwise sterile meetings." Appropriately enough, the specific joke that Tomsen chooses to illustrate Khalis's sense of humor is darkly anti-Shi'a. See Tomsen, 306. Yunus Khalis was famously cantankerous and prone to speak his mind about controversial issues, qualities that did not endear him to his enemies, but which just as certainly make his biographies more entertaining to read. For his tirade against Taliban policies that he disagreed with, see Muhammad (2007), 105–107. For his dismissal of a Pakistani 'alim's (religious scholar) ideas about politics in a conversation at Mullah Omar's house, see ibid., 109–110. For an amusing depiction of Khalis publicly upbraiding a young Arab who tried to argue with him about the legal acceptability of listening to music, see ibid., 207–208. For an account of Khalis storming out of a meeting with a Pakistani official in disgust (and before getting any lunch), see Tomsen, 472.

[23] Keep in mind that his inclusion in Shohrat Nangyal's monumental book on mujahidin writers *Blood on the Pen* is predicated on the idea that Khalis was an important jihadi writer. Nangyal discusses some of Khalis's publications on page 156 and includes a large section of Khalis's autobiography on the preceding pages. See Nangyal, 146–156. Din Muhammad's book begins with a discussion of Khalis's poetry and prose writings and includes fifteen pages of Khalis's poems. See Muhammad (2007), 10–25.

[24] He edited several different publishing ventures in the 1950s, including *The Beam of Light (Wrranga)* and *The Message of Truth (Payam-e Haq)*. He was later involved in putting together an Islamic political publication called *Gahiz* in the late 1960s.

show on Kabul Radio for several years.[25] His various protégés and commanders from the Soviet jihad remain among the most powerful men still living in eastern Afghanistan, and Khalis continues to be a relevant figure in his home province of Nangarhar even after his death in 2006.[26] As a prominent and highly literate member of a society in which illiteracy is still pervasive, Khalis's life and writings give us a window into the otherwise almost illegible world of the political elite in the eastern Pashtun tribes around Nangarhar. And as his biographies reveal, in the mid-1990s the life of this political elite was dominated by the Eastern Shura based in Jalalabad.

In the midst of the Afghan Civil War, there were small pockets of relative quiet. Due to the admittedly self-interested efforts of the Eastern Shura, the area around Jalalabad was one of the safest and most prosperous in all Afghanistan during this period. Paradoxically, it was this relative peace in Nangarhar Province that allowed Usama bin Ladin to contemplate Jalalabad as a region of refuge when he fled Sudan. Yunus Khalis and his former commanders such as 'Abd al-Qadir played essential roles in creating and maintaining a relatively peaceful environment in Nangarhar in the 1990s. An investigation of Khalis's life offers a unique perspective on the way that former mujahidin leaders based in Jalalabad used a multilateral shura to negotiate peaceful resolutions to certain regional conflicts during one of the darkest and most violent periods in the region's history.

Ultimately, the Eastern Shura was able to keep Nangarhar Province "open for business,"[27] but it also appears to have had little interest in pursuing and eliminating

---

[25] Khalis hosted a radio program in which he gave interpretations of the Qur'an (*tafsir*) in Kabul for several years.

[26] Commanders from Khalis's party include the current head of the Haqqani Network (Jalaluddin Haqqani), a former vice president of Afghanistan (Haji 'Abd al-Qadir), the former governor of Kabul and Nangarhar Provinces (Haji Din Muhammad) and many other important figures. The housing development that Khalis built and named Najm al-Jihad is now more commonly known under his name as "Khalis Families" or "Khalis Colony." This large development is situated immediately south of Jalalabad and houses thousands of people.

[27] Semple, Michael, interview by Kevin Bell. *Unpublished Interview with Michael Semple* (2012 September).. This turn of phrase is suggestive of the way that commerce through the Jalalabad Airport and the Torkham Gate gave local leaders an economic stake in maintaining a relatively peaceful province. Many of the goods transported through Nangarhar during this period were shipped duty-free to Nangarhar from Karachi. This material was eventually destined for Pakistani markets. Taking this circuitous route allowed importers in Pakistan to avoid tariffs and duties at the port in Karachi. Once the goods arrived in Nangarhar, the material could then be smuggled back into Pakistan for sale at an enormous profit. The

violent jihadist organizations such as the one that killed four UN officials in an ambush near Jalalabad on 1 February 1993.[28] And as Dipali Mukhopadhyay has demonstrated in her work, the intense rivalries held in check by the Eastern Shura until late 1996 burst into the open again after the fall of the Taliban in 2001.[29] By improving our understanding of Yunus Khalis we can begin to historicize one of the most persistent myths of al-Qa'ida's connection to the Afghan mujahidin while filling the gaps in our knowledge of how political power has been managed in the strategically vital region around Nangarhar Province. In the process insights can be gained into the fascinating life of an important east Afghan political and intellectual figure who was intimately involved in Afghanistan's reactions to and negotiations with modernity. There is too much at stake in the world's understanding of recent Afghan history for us to continue to ignore the available primary sources about politics in the Afghan frontier. With that in mind, this analysis will begin with a discussion of what these sources say about Yunus Khalis's life up to the beginning of the Soviet-Afghan War in 1979.

---

profitability of this activity gave everyone a stake in maintaining the security of the Khyber Pass and the Jalalabad Airport.

[28] U.S. Department of State. "Department of State Publication 10136." (Washington, DC, 1994).

[29] See especially Dipali Mukhopadhyay's chapter on Gul Agha Sherzai: Dipali Mukhopadhyay. *Warlords, Strongman Governors and State Building in Afghanistan.* (New York: Cambridge University Press, forthcoming), 114–170.

Yunus Khalis's Life and Career up to the Soviet-Afghan War

Khalis's Education and Early Years

The man best known today as Yunus Khalis (d. 2006) was born Muhammad Yunus in a village near Gandamak in Nangarhar Province to a family of the Khugiani tribe in 1920.[30] Yunus Khalis was home schooled, and after his father's death he began to take lessons from his uncle 'Abd al-Razeq.[31] He continued his education at local towns such as Kami, but before long his studies sent him further afield to Jalalabad, and eventually, to the famous Dar al-'Ulum Deoband with his elder brother.[32] While there, Khalis's brother became sick, and an acquaintance recommended that they travel back north to study with a Deoband graduate who was then teaching at Akora Khattak near Peshawar.[33] They followed this advice, and thus Khalis became a student of Mawlana 'Abd al-Haq Haqqani, the founder of the Dar al-'Ulum Haqqaniyya.[34]

Western sources rarely discuss Khalis's education, but when it is mentioned, authors usually focus on his attendance at the now infamous Dar al-'Ulum Haqqaniyya.[35]

---

[30] Ahmadzai, 4; and Muhammad (2007), 1. For those interested in his genealogy, his family was from the Nabi Khel sublineage of the Ibrahim Khel branch of the Khugianis. It is not yet clear when he took the name "Khalis." Apparently he was not yet authoring articles under that name in 1968, but by the time that he was involved in the jihad he was known as Yunus Khalis. See the final pages of Khalis (2002), and Nangyal, 149.

[31] Nangyal, 149.

[32] Muhammad (2007), 1. The Dar al-'Ulum Deoband, which is often called the Deoband Madrasa, is one of the most important institutions of Islamic learning in the world, and it has had a dramatic impact on the interpretation and reception of forms of modernism among the community of Islamic scholars in South Asia. Although Muhammad Qasim Zaman's book *The Ulama in Contemporary Islam* is not primarily about the Dar al-'Ulum Deoband, it offers a good overview of the effect that this institution has had on South Asian religious discourse. See Muhammad Qasim Zaman. *The Ulama in Contemporary Islam.* (Princeton, NJ: Princeton University Press, 2002).

[33] Muhammad (2007), 1; the unstated implication being that this was much closer to home, and that the instruction would be good.

[34] Muhammad (2007), 2. 'Abd al-Haq Haqqani gave his name to the madrasa he eventually founded in 1947, and it is from the Dar al-'Ulum Haqqaniyya that Jalaluddin Haqqani took his nickname when he graduated. Jalaluddin Haqqani is now best known as the founder of the eponymous Haqqani Network, and he was one of Yunus Khalis's most important commanders during the Soviet-Afghan War. This madrasa is sometimes referred to in English as the Haqqaniyya Madrasa.

[35] It is not common for authors to discuss Khalis's education, but where they do, they usually list Haqqaniyya as his alma mater. For a typical example, see Dorronsoro, Gilles. *Revolution Unending: Afghanistan: 1979 to present.* (New York: Columbia University Press, 2005), 152.

Unfortunately, this is not quite historically accurate. It is true that Yunus Khalis studied with 'Abd al-Haq Haqqani at Akora, but Khalis completed his education in 1941 and returned to Afghanistan before 'Abd al-Haq Haqqani founded the Dar al-'Ulum Haqqaniyya in 1947.[36] While it is known that Yunus Khalis studied the sayings of the prophet Muhammad (*hadith*) under 'Abd al-Haq Haqqani,[37] his education in the frontier appears to have been far broader than this.

Khalis traveled throughout Swat and Buner districts and the Bajaur and Dir tribal agencies to learn from the most famous frontier 'ulama of the time.[38] He received a traditional education in logic, rhetoric, grammar, philosophy, religious law (*fiqh*) and the interpretation of the Qur'an (*tafsir*).[39] It is implicit in all of this that he learned Arabic. Not all students of the private madrasa system in South Asia graduate with a proficiency in this language beyond what is absolutely necessary for liturgical and ritual purposes.[40] However, Khalis translated books from Arabic,[41] wrote some of his original work in Arabic[42] and spoke it well enough to converse without an interpreter.[43]

This education in the private madrasa system set Khalis apart from many of the other men who eventually became leaders in the mujahidin movement[44] and connected Khalis with a group of Haqqaniyya alumni who would become critical to his fight against the Soviets later in life. But these links would only become militarily relevant much later, and when Yunus Khalis returned to Afghanistan around 1941 he spent his

---

[36] Ahmadzai, 6.

[37] Ahmadzai, 6.

[38] Muhammad (2007), 2; and Ahmadzai, 5.

[39] Ahmadzai, 6.

[40] Zaman notes that speaking and writing proficiency in Arabic "was said to be beyond the abilities of most graduates of the Indian madrasas." See Zaman, 71. He also points out that some groups, like the Nadwat al-'Ulama, explicitly sought to reform the madrasa system in South Asia so that graduates would be more functionally proficient in Arabic. This was not always successful, but Yunus Khalis appears to have gained a good grasp of Arabic through his education.

[41] Ahmadzai, 81.

[42] Ahmadzai, 84–85. Khalis wrote *The Explanation of the Creed of al-Tahawiyah* in Arabic before translating it into Pashto. See Ahmadzai, 84–88. Din Muhammad also notes that Khalis composed some of his poetry in Arabic. See Muhammad (2007), 9.

[43] Scheuer (2011), 105.

[44] The majority of these leaders were educated in state-run schools in Afghanistan and Egypt. Of the seven mujahidin party leaders, only Khalis and Muhammad Nabi Muhammadi were educated in the private madrasa system (both were connected to the Dar al-'Ulum Haqqaniyya).

time studying, giving sermons and teaching unofficially at the Najm al-Madaris school in Nangarhar beginning in 1943.[45] The year 1949 proved to be a time of dramatic change for Khalis, and by the end of it he was married[46] and had moved to Kabul to teach at a professional school for future judges called the Dar al-Quza.[47] Yunus Khalis would remain on the faculty there for two years until he was hired by the government in 1952 to run a new show on Kabul Radio interpreting the Qur'an.[48]

Khalis's Political Awakening and Media Activity

It was during his long tenure at Kabul Radio that the first hint of Khalis engaging in an act of political resistance emerges. When the Suez Crisis erupted in 1956, Yunus Khalis took the opportunity while on the air to call on all Muslim nations to "stand with the people of Egypt" against the aggression of Britain, France and Israel.[49] Khalis' boss, under pressure from his superiors in the government, cut the transmission without even informing Khalis that he had gone off the air. This is certainly a colorful story, but it seems more likely to have been an isolated incident than evidence of Khalis' taking an active stand against the government in Kabul in the 1950s. After all, he still had his show at Kabul Radio for at least two years after the Suez Crisis, and in 1958 he was appointed by the Ministry of Information and Culture to be the director of what may have been Afghanistan's first Islamic magazine, *The Message of Truth (Payam-e Haq)*.[50]

---

[45] Ahmadzai, 6, 9-10. The Najm al-Madaris is one of the oldest state madrasas in Afghanistan. It was founded in the reign of Nadir Shah in 1931.

[46] Muhammad (2007), 2.

[47] Ahmadzai, 9-10.

[48] Ahmadzai, 10-11. It is not always clear if Khalis ceased working at one position when he moved to another, but in any event, it does not appear that he spent very many years working at the Dar al-Qaza since it receives scant mention in the biographies.

[49] Muhammad (2007), 31-32. The Suez Crisis was partially a result of Egypt's 1956 nationalization of the Suez Canal, and it resulted in a major diplomatic and military loss for Britain and France. Presumably, King Zaher Shah's government did not want to stir up trouble for Afghanistan's Western allies and shut off Khalis's radio broadcast in an effort to keep him from causing too much trouble.

[50] Ahmadzai, 11–12. Relatively little is known about *The Message of Truth* except that it apparently began to be published in 1955, three years before Khalis's tenure as director began in 1958. It was a government publication affiliated with the Ministry of Information and Culture at one point, but with the Ministry of Guidance and Pilgrimage at other points. Little information is available about its contents, other authors involved in the publication, or the intended audience. As the earliest known publication of its kind, it is a sharp loss for scholarship of modern Afghanistan that this publication is currently unstudied. Partial archives of this material appear in Firestone Library at Princeton University.

Khalis's involvement in print journalism marked an important shift in his professional life, but he was not a newcomer to other print media and would return to publishing repeatedly in the years after he left his job at *The Message of Truth*. Around 1954 he published a book of his own called *Religious Pearls* and a translation of a book by the 19th century French social psychologist Gustave Le Bon under the title *Religion and Human Society*.[51] Khalis's publication credits would eventually include works in a large variety of genres. He published books for use by students such as *The Spirit of Islam* and *The Explanation of the Creed of al-Tahawiya*, and he apparently developed a system to help young children learn to read the Qur'an.[52] He also wrote volumes of poetry,[53] and at least one translation of Sayyid Qutb's work.[54] Of course, it is hard to know how widely circulated these books really were. They were generally printed in small runs,[55] but this tells us almost nothing about their possible impact since popular books disseminated in hand-written copies to the right readers can have an enormous influence compared

---

[51] See Muhammad (2007), 5. Khalis's work on this translation is especially noteworthy because of the well-known influence of Gustave Le Bon's ideas of crowd psychology and racial theories on European Fascism. Khalis is known to have held extreme views about Shi'a, but there are few textual clues that offer insight into this part of his thinking. In general we find none of the rabidly anti-Shi'a polemics in Khalis's written works that many accounts ascribe to him based on face-to-face interactions, and it is not known if the racially charged portions of Le Bon's work were what primarily interested Khalis. If a copy of Khalis's translation of Le Bon is ever found, however, it could offer some clues to the intellectual underpinning of Khalis's stance against the Shi'a. Part of the obstacle to this line of inquiry is that the title given for Khalis's translation does not match any of Le Bon's known titles. It could be a rendering of either *L'Homme et les Sociétés, Leurs Origines et Leur Histoire* or *La Civilisation des Arabes*. Ahmadzai gives the author of the book as Muhammad al-Bahi al-Khuli, a Muslim Brotherhood 'alim, and says that Khalis translated the book from Arabic. See Ahmadzai, 109–111. Possibly the book was written in French by Le Bon, translated into Arabic by al-Khuli and then translated into Pashto by Khalis. In any event, it would make some sense if Khalis read this work in Arabic, since otherwise there is no evidence that Khalis knew French.

[52] *The Spirit of Islam* is undated, but appears to have been published around 1979, and *The Explanation of the Creed of al-Tahawiyah* was published in 1987. Din Muhammad briefly mentions Khalis's work on materials for early childhood education in reading the Qur'an. See Muhammad (2007), 7.

[53] The most recent of these was published in 2002 and is a collection of his other previous publications in verse.

[54] He published a translation of *Islam and Social Justice* in 1960. Ahmadzai claims that a mutual acquaintance told him that Khalis also wrote a translation of Qutb's monumental work *In the Shadows of the Qur'an*. Unfortunately, as of Ahmadzai's publication in 2006, this translation was still a rumor. See Ahmadzai, 111–112.

[55] Ahmadzai conveniently includes notes about the publication run of Khalis's books where he knows the numbers. See Ahmadzai, 81–114.

with state-sponsored books printed in large quantities.[56] That is partly what makes Khalis's role as the head of *The Message of Truth* and other journals so interesting. This kind of work may have increased his exposure to the writings of his contemporaries and vice versa, and it also helps to make his professional and intellectual connections more easily visible to us today.

While directing *The Message of Truth*, Khalis received articles and letters from professors, teachers, and students in Herat, Kunduz, Mazar-e Sharif, Nangarhar, and Kabul.[57] Through his involvement with this explicitly Islamic publication, Khalis was developing a network of connections to 'ulama and writers throughout the late 1950s. His role as curator of the intellectual output of many of his peers was made all the more important and sensitive because of the interest that the government censors took in publications like *The Message of Truth* that could be a potential source of political resistance to Kabul.[58] His efforts to balance this delicate position must have been at least partially successful; he was soon placed in charge of a second publication called *The Beam of Light* (*Wrangah*) operated out of Gardez in Paktia Province.[59]

Khalis left journalism temporarily when a serious illness prevented him from working, but by 1960 he was already back in Kabul teaching at the Dar al-'Ulum 'Arabi.[60] In the 1960s Khalis's political views began to come under increasing scrutiny by the government, and he was repeatedly fired and sent to teach at progressively less prestigious and more peripheral schools.[61] At some point he tired of the transfers and

---

[56] For more on the impact of works disseminated partially through handwritten copies on the Muslim Youth, see David Edwards. "Summoning Muslims: Print, Politics, and Religious Ideology in Afghanistan." (*The Journal of Asian Studies* 52, no. 3 (1993)), 609-628; and David Edwards. "Print Islam: Media and Religious Revolution in Afghanistan." (*Social Movements: An Anthropological Reader*, edited by June Nash, 99-116. Malden: Blackwell, 2005).

[57] Ahmadzai, 12.

[58] Ahmadzai, 12.

[59] Ahmadzai, 13–14. Although little is known about *The Message of Truth*, almost nothing at all is known about *The Beam of Light*. If the chronology presented by the biographies is correct, *The Beam of Light* must have been published during the period before Yunus Khalis left journalism and then returned to teach at the Dar al-'Ulum al-'Arabi in Kabul in 1960. Like *The Message of Truth*, *The Beam of Light* appears to have been an Islamic publication, which operated under the auspices of the Ministry of Information and Culture.

[60] Ahmadzai, 14. The Dar al-'Ulum 'Arabi in Kabul is the oldest and most prominent state madrasa in Afghanistan. It was founded by Amir Amanulllah in 1920.

[61] Ahmadzai, 14.

ideological interference, and he quit teaching at government schools entirely.[62] While the primary sources are silent about Khalis's activities during most of the 1960s, the narrative thread of his life can be picked up again in 1966, when Khalis helped to form an "Islamic group" in Nangarhar.[63] Although it is unknown if this is the same group that Khalis cofounded with the journalist Minhajuddin Gahiz, it seems likely that these two men were already connected by this point.[64]

The Growth of an Islamic Political Opposition in Afghanistan

There was a flurry of quiet Islamist organizing activity led by 'ulama, professors and students in all of the major population centers of Afghanistan in the 1960s. In Kabul, much of this activity centered around Professor Ghulam Niazi, who had returned to Afghanistan in the 1950s to teach after receiving a Master's Degree from the famous al-Azhar University in Egypt.[65] Professor Ghulam Niazi founded an underground Islamic organization in 1965,[66] and by 1969 this group had given birth to the "Muslim Youth" and prepared the way for what would become the first mujahidin political party in the 1970s.[67]

---

[62] Ahmadzai, 15-16.

[63] Muhammad (2007), 26.

[64] Minhajuddin Gahiz was an important writer and political activist who helped to cofound a mysterious group called the Hizb al-Tawabin, and eventually created the journal *Gahiz* to help counteract the influence of the leftist publications, which were then becoming increasingly prominent in Afghanistan.

[65] Al-Azhar is one of the most prestigious religious universities in the Muslim world; students are often willing to travel thousands of miles to study there. It is often assumed because of the activities of the Muslim Brotherhood around al-Azhar in the mid-20th century that the Afghans who traveled to study there were influenced by the Brotherhood's ideology. In the case of Niazi and several other Afghan scholars who studied at al-Azhar, this appears to be essentially correct.

[66] Ahmadzai, 25–26.

[67] The Muslim Youth was an organization largely made up of Kabul University students interested in becoming active in politics, and it was connected to Professor Ghulam Niazi's other political circles. The ideological orientation of this group can effectively be termed "Islamist," in part because of the influence on this group of Niazi's circle of professors who were educated at al-Azhar University in Egypt and had ties to the Muslim Brotherhood. This group eventually became much more radical than the more secretive group of lecturers like 'Abd al-Rab Rasul Sayyaf and Burhanuddin Rabbani, and the Muslim Youth formed the backbone of Gulbuddin Hekmatyar's base of support when he built his own political party later in the 1970s. Khalis's eldest son was apparently active in an offshoot of this movement operating in northern Afghanistan, and Khalis frequently met with students during the time period when the Muslim Youth was becoming more widespread and powerful. David Edwards even says that Khalis was "aligned with the Muslim Youth Organization in the early 1970s." See David Edwards. *Before Taliban: Genealogies of the Afghan Jihad*. (Berkeley and Los Angeles: University of California Press, 2002), 247. For a

It is important to keep in mind that the focus on Professor Niazi in many histories of the earliest stages of the mujahidin movement is in part a reflection of the later fame and influence of several important leaders who were involved in his circles in Kabul. These men included the world-famous Panjshiri commander Ahmad Shah Massoud; Burhanuddin Rabbani of the Jami'at-e Islami party; 'Abd al-Rab Rasul Sayyaf who eventually led the Ittihad-e Islami party; and Gulbuddin Hekmatyar, whose clashes with Massoud were one of the main drivers of the devastation of the Afghan Civil War. Of these, Rabbani and Hekmatyar struggled directly over the question of who was best suited to follow in Niazi's footsteps and lead the Islamist movement in Afghanistan.[68] But aside from the clearly justifiable interest in tracing the intellectual and political histories of these four important leaders, scholars also tend to focus on Professor Niazi's circles at least partially because there is so little available information about the activists from this period who were not based in Kabul.[69] However, this reasoning may focus too much on scholars and their impact on readings of history without accounting for the tremendous efforts made by the various Afghan actors to warp depictions of the history of 20th century Afghanistan to fit their own political agenda.

The Jami'at-e Islami and Hizb-e Islami (Gulbuddin) parties were highly successful at shaping accounts of the origins of the mujahidin movement to advance their own interests. These two parties split dramatically along ethnic and generational lines and

---

glimpse at Khalis's own somewhat complex views on the youth in Afghanistan in the early 1970s, see his article "From the Youths Who Are Appointed by Political Events," Khalis, 40–43.

[68] David Edwards gives an excellent account of how Gulbuddin Hekmatyar and Burhanuddin Rabbani struggled over who was most fit to assume the mantle of Professor Ghulam Niazi's legacy. See Edwards (2002), 237–240. There is no question that Niazi was an important figure in the history of the mujahidin movements in Afghanistan, this report simply seeks to point out some of the reasons for the overall primacy of place given to Niazi in discussions of the early history of the Islamists in Afghanistan.

[69] There are important exceptions to this trend. Thomas Ruttig has done interesting work on various Islamist movements from around Afghanistan, including the Khuddam al-Furqan. This movement was drawn from 'ulama close to Ibrahim Mujaddidi, and does not appear to have been based primarily in Kabul. See Thomas Ruttig. "The Ex-Taleban on the High Peace Council: A renewed role for the Khuddam ul-Furqan?" (*The Afghan Analysts Network.* 2010 October). http://aan-afghanistan.com/index.asp?id=1248.; and Thomas Ruttig. "Islamists, Leftists – and a Void in the Center." (*Konrad-Adenauer-Stiftung - Afghanistan Office.* 2006 27-November), 8. http://www.kas.de/afghanistan/en/publications/9674/. Even so, the scholarly emphasis on Niazi in the narrative of the history of the mujahidin is striking. Reading Mullah Zaeef's biography also offers a markedly different and non-Peshawar/Kabul-focused version of events during this period. See Mullah Zaeef. *My Life with the Taliban.* (London: C Hurst & Co., 2011).

thus mirror larger divisions within the mujahidin. Jam'iat-e Islami became the only Sunni mujahidin party to include a high proportion of non-Pashtun members, while Gulbuddin Hekmatyar's Hizb-e Islami was formed from the core membership of the Muslim Youth. Hekmatyar's following was generally younger, more politically radical and more willing to take sometimes foolish risks in the early days of the mujahidin movement.[70] It should be no surprise that Rabbani and Hekmatyar's efforts to lay claim to the legacy of Professor Niazi have produced a group of sources for Western scholars, which emphasize Niazi's importance to the development of the mujahidin movement in Afghanistan.

Niazi has an important role to play in any history of the mujahidin, but his group at Kabul University was not the only politically active Islamic organization in Afghanistan in the late 1960s. The primary sources abound with stories of clandestine meetings of activists where leaders such as Yunus Khalis, sometimes joined by the Sufi leader Sibghatullah Mujaddidi,[71] would discuss Islam, socialism and politics with teachers, professionals and young people.[72] Sibghatullah Mujaddidi would eventually go on to create his own mujahidin political party by mobilizing his contacts in Afghan Sufi networks.[73] Certainly, some of the gatherings attended by Khalis and Mujaddidi took place at Kabul University, however these kinds of informal groups also met in Kunduz, Nangarhar and many other locations.[74]

Even while they were distinct from the Kabul Islamists to some extent, their purpose appears to have been the same: to awaken the population to socialism's threat to their way of life, to give attendees useful rhetorical tools to help combat leftists in their schools and towns and, as the movements developed, to help organize and connect the

---

[70] This is especially apparent in Hekmatyar's involvement in the disastrous 1975 attempt to stage a coup d'état in Afghanistan.

[71] Mujaddidi was already an internationally recognized leader of a Sufi order, and later became the leader of the Jebha-ye Nejat-e Milli, one of the seven Sunni mujahidin political parties.

[72] Muhammad (2007), 26.

[73] For further discussion of Mujaddidi's family and its influence on the early directions taken by the Islamic resistance movements in Afghanistan, see Olivier Roy. *Islam and Resistance in Afghanistan*. 2nd. Translated by Gwydir St. First Edition. (New York: Cambridge University Press, 1990), 47. Ibrahim Mujaddidi was closely involved in the development of the Khuddam al-Furqan organization as well. See Ruttig (2010), 6; and Ruttig (2006), 8.

[74] Muhammad (2007), 26–27. By the early 1970s it appears that Mujaddidi was no longer welcome at meetings at which Hekmatyar and some of the other Islamists were holding court.

members.[75] Surprisingly enough, some of these early gatherings actually included socialist activists and thinkers such as Suleiman Layeq.[76] Of course it quickly became impossible to have meetings in which Islamists and Leftists both took part: Gulbuddin Hekmatyar served a jail sentence for murdering a Maoist student in 1972.[77] As these discussion groups spread to different cities and radicalized, they gave birth to different kinds of organizations with similar political goals. Two of the most interesting of these organizations were the short-lived Hizb al-Tawabin of Nangarhar and the aforementioned Muslim Youth, created at Kabul University from among the younger members of Professor Niazi's circles.

The history of the Muslim Youth and Gulbuddin Hekmatyar's involvement with it are well known. The creation of the Muslim Youth in 1969 merely made explicit some of the previously hidden divisions in Niazi's circles between students like Hekmatyar and professors like Sayyaf and Rabbani.[78] Many of these activists would later go on to become the leaders of separate mujahidin political parties. But in spite of their already sharpening ideological differences, many of the most important members of the nascent mujahidin movement were writing under pseudonyms for the same Hizb al-Tawabin publication, a journal named *Gahiz* (Dawn).[79]

Minhajuddin Gahiz created an organization called the Hizb al-Tawabin in 1965,[80] which would go on to publish the *Gahiz* journal from 1968 to 1972.[81] Yunus Khalis was a

---

[75] These purposes are rarely outlined, but the topics of discussion help to clarify what the purposes of the meetings were. Din Muhammad includes numerous examples of these kinds of gatherings in his section entitled "Mawlawi Khalis's Political Life." See Muhammad (2007), 26-43. The earliest meetings of Niazi's group are described as reading groups meant to train young men on how to counteract leftist ideology. See Fazal al Rahim Khan Marwat, Sayyid Vaqar 'Ali Shah, et al. *Afghanistan and the Frontier*. (Peshawar: Emjay Books International, 1993), 9.

[76] Muhammad (2007), 143.

[77] Coll, 113.

[78] See Edwards (2002), 225–278.

[79] Marwat Shah, et al., 5–6. Unlike the other titles of publications in this report, we will retain the title of this magazine as *Gahiz* instead of translating it.

[80] The organization centered on Minhajuddin Gahiz and his eponymous publication is peripheral to most Western histories of the mujahidin, and is best described in Ahmadzai, 25-26. Din Muhammad mentions that Khalis founded an Islamic society in Nangarhar in 1966, and states that this organization expanded and eventually took on the responsibility of publishing *Gahiz*. It seems likely that this organization was connected to the Hizb al-Tawabin, but more research is needed to disambiguate this group from the other informal political circles active at the time. See Muhammad (2007), 26.

founding member of the Hizb al-Tawabin,[82] and he was involved in the publication of *Gahiz* from the very beginning.[83] Although the Hizb al-Tawabin never became a well-known political party, it evidently played an important role in connecting some of the most important mujahidin leaders to one another. In 1984, when Burhanuddin Rabbani wished to conduct some important political business with Qazi Hussain Ahmad,[84] he brought Yunus Khalis to the meeting with him on the basis of Khalis's old connection to Hussain Ahmad through the long-defunct Hizb al-Tawabin.[85]

The level of involvement in the Hizb al-Tawabin's *Gahiz* journal by the men who would eventually become leaders of the various mujahidin political parties is striking: Minhajuddin Gahiz apparently turned to Sibghatullah Mujaddidi for the financial support needed to get his publication off the ground, and Burhanuddin Rabbani supported *Gahiz* from the beginning.[86] Hekmatyar himself admitted to submitting several articles for publication in *Gahiz* under various pseudonyms even though he claimed that the journal was not very popular among young people.[87] It is not yet known whether the three other future Sunni mujahidin party leaders (Sayyid Ahmed Gailani, Sayyaf and Muhammad Nabi Muhammadi) had any involvement in *Gahiz*. Even so, it is remarkable that four of the seven eventual party leaders contributed articles or funds to an Islamic magazine at a time when the splits between the various factions were making it increasingly difficult for some of them to even sit together in the same room.

Yunus Khalis was busy with a variety of projects during the time in which he collaborated with Minhajuddin on the *Gahiz* publication. In the space of two years he

---

[81] Ahmadzai gives the dates of Khalis's first and last articles in *Gahiz* as 1968 and 1972. We will take those as a baseline for the print-run of *Gahiz* until the actual magazine can be found. See Ahmadzai, 88.

[82] This is described as an organization "against obscenity" in one source. See Marwat, Shah, et al., 226. Other founding members included Gahiz himself, Mawlawi 'Abd al-Rab Ahedi Wardak, Ahmad Khan Tarjiman, and Sayyid 'Abd al-Ahad 'Asharti. 'Abd al-Ahad is described as "the highest ranking member and a skilled writer." See Ahmadzai, 25-26.

[83] See the first article that Khalis published in *Gahiz* in Khalis, 1-3.

[84] Qazi Hussain Ahmad is a prominent religious scholar and political figure in Pakistan. He was the amir of the Pakistani Jami'at-e Islami political party from 1987 to 2008.

[85] This anecdote reveals something about Ahmadzai's otherwise unknown role during the jihad. See Ahmadzai, 115–116.

[86] Marwat, Shah, et al., 5–6. Din Muhammad even casually refers to *Gahiz* as being under the leadership of Sibghatullah Mujaddidi. See Muhammad (2007), 141.

[87] Marwat, Shah, et al., 6.

went on the Haj,[88] wrote at least one new book,[89] remained publicly active enough to speak out in defense of destitute mullahs before an assembly in Nangarhar[90] and took a position conducting research at a media group in Kabul.[91] He did all of this while regularly contributing articles to *Gahiz*. During the 1970's, the Afghan state's security apparatus dramatically tightened its control over anti-government political activity. With that increased attention from the government, the period of relative government tolerance for the various Islamic organizations and resistance movements would not last much longer.[92] Around the time in 1972 that Burhanuddin Rabbani took control of the nascent Jami'at-e Islami[93] from Professor Ghulam Niazi, Minhajuddin Gahiz was killed.[94] Soon after Gahiz's assassination,[95] Muhammad Daoud Khan staged a coup and overthrew Muhammad Zaher Shah—the last king of Afghanistan.

---

[88] Ahmadzai, 19.

[89] The one book that we can definitely date to this period was entitled *Wisdom, Imitation, and Worldly Benefits*. See Ahmadzai, 91–92, for a synopsis of the book. Ahmadzai is very critical of this work, not least because Khalis glowingly refers to Dr. Gustave Le Bon, whom Ahmadzai sees as a communist and a wicked man. It is not yet known which portions of Le Bon's work most interested Khalis, but it is likely that he was familiar with Le Bon's influential ideas about race. Future work is needed to determine if this is connected to Khalis's thoughts on the Shi'a, especially the Hazaras. Khalis also eventually wrote a guidebook for Pashtuns going on the Haj called *The Guide to the Haj*. It is not known when he published this work, but it seems likely that he wrote it sometime after his own travel to Mecca between 1968 and 1974. Ahmadzai mentions it briefly. See Ahmadzai, 83.

[90] Muhammad (2007), 32–33.

[91] Ahmadzai, 19–20; and Muhammad (2007), 2–3.

[92] Between 1964 and 1973 Afghanistan was going through a period of accelerated political and social change. There were many possible futures imaginable for Afghanistan during this time, when King Zaher Shah approved a constitutional monarchy and a new democratically elected parliament. Unfortunately, radical leftist ideology was also strengthened in this period of relative democratic growth. The mujahidin were largely a reaction to this increasing Marxist-Leninist presence, and it was these Leninist-style political parties (including what became the Muslim Youth) that ultimately played a decisive role in determining Afghanistan's future in the early 1970s.

[93] This organization had gone through many names, including Ikhwan al-Muslimin-e Afghanistan (Muslim Brothers of Afghanistan), Jami'at-e 'Ulama-ye Afghanistan (not to be confused with the separate government controlled Jami'at-e 'Ulama), and Jami'at-e Islami-ye Afghanistan. A good account of the early structure of the group that Niazi passed on to Rabbani is given in *Afghanistan and the Fronter*. See Marwat, Shah, et al., 9-13.

[94] Ahmadzai, 25; Marwat, Shah et al., 7. These two sources differ by a few weeks about the date of his death, but they are close enough that there seems little reason to doubt that Minhajuddin Gahiz was killed in the fall of 1972.

[95] Khalis's associates seem to have believed that Gahiz was assassinated, and Din Muhammad refers to him as a martyr (*shahid*). See Muhammad (2007), 26. Ahmadzai also calls him a martyr and goes so far as to claim that he was killed by Russians of the KGB in August of 1972. See Ahmadzai, 26. Whether or not

Daoud Khan's 1973 Coup and the Movement of Mujahidin Leaders to Pakistan

The consequences of Daoud's leftist coup in 1973 have been far-reaching, but the immediate result was a dramatic crackdown on the Islamic resistance. Within a year many activists had been arrested, including Professor Ghulam Niazi and Yunus Khalis's eldest son, Mawlawi Muhammad Nasim.[96] Muhammad Nasim had evidently drawn attention to himself by publicly denouncing a leftist sermon delivered by the governor of Balkh during a Friday prayer service in 1973, and within a few days Nasim was arrested.[97] Both he and Professor Ghulam Niazi would eventually die in prison.[98] Unsurprisingly, Yunus Khalis was also being hunted by the government, and he fled to Peshawar in 1974.[99]

David Edwards reports that Yunus Khalis kept a low profile in his initial years around Peshawar.[100] Khalis was probably careful as long as his son was alive in prison and much of his family remained in Afghanistan, but the case for his lack of political activity at the time can be overstated. While he did not make a play for leadership of Jami'at-e Islami or the Muslim Youth, Khalis was an active participant in one of the first gatherings of the key mujahidin leadership in exile.

In 1974 Burhanuddin Rabbani invited a group of mujahidin leaders to his home in a suburb of Peshawar for a conference.[101] The list of leaders in attendance is impressive: Gulbuddin Hekmatyar, Yunus Khalis, Mawlawi Jamil al-Rahman,[102] Qazi Amin

---

the KGB was involved, it seems very likely that this was a political assassination given Gahiz's known antileftist political publications and agitation.

[96] Ahmadzai, 30–31.

[97] Ahmadzai, 30–31.

[98] Niazi was briefly released in 1973 after Daoud's coup, but he was later rearrested and died in prison.

[99] Ahmadzai, 32.

[100] See Edwards (2002), 247–248.

[101] Muhammad (2007), 33–35.

[102] Jamil al-Rahman met occasionally with Khalis, and although Din Muhammad claims that Jamil al-Rahman was one of the founding members of Hizb-e Islami (Khalis), it seems likely that Jamil al-Rahman was more closely involved with Hekmatyar. Habib al-Rahman, a former commander for Jamil al-Rahman, claims that Jamil al-Rahman was involved with Hizb-e Islami (Gulbuddin) until 1984 when he cut his ties to all of the mujahidin parties and went home. Some time later (around 1988) Jamil al-Rahman created the party known as "Jama'at al-Da'wa ila al-Sunna wal-Qur'an" (The Society of Invitation to the Sunna and the Qur'an). It was with this Jama'at al-Da'wa party that Jamil al-Rahman

Waqad,[103] Mawlawi Nasrullah Mansur,[104] Mawlawi Jalaluddin Haqqani,[105] Mati'ullah Khan Wali Khel,[106] and Haji Din Muhammad.[107] Khalis showed up to the meeting with nothing but a shawl and a hand ax,[108] and apparently asked uncomfortably specific questions about what sort of leadership and planning goals the group was prepared to put forward.[109] Din Muhammad eventually became the deputy chief of Khalis's political party. In his account of this meeting, Din Muhammad ascribes an uncannily prophetic line of reasoning to his former boss. Khalis allegedly asked the gathering "if Daoud Khan gave the government into your hands, who would be the leaders?" The response was laughter, and a fuming Yunus Khalis supposedly responded that if the group could not agree on this issue now, then the nation would be bathed in blood when they came into power.[110]

---

would eventually hold independent elections in Kunar and create a separate Salafi state in 1991. He led this state until he was assassinated later that same year. Habib al-Rahman. *Unpublished Author Interview with Former Jama'at al-Da'wa Commander Habib al-Rahman*. Edited by Kevin Bell, translated by Anonymous and Kevin Bell. (Kabul, (March 30, 2013)). Peter Tomsen offers one of the only English language accounts of the Islamic Emirate in Kunar. See Tomsen, 367.

[103] Qazi Amin would eventually become the leader of the first version of the Hizb-e Islami, and later would be an important leader in Gulbuddin Hekmatyar's Hizb-e Islami. Edwards includes a lot of interesting information about Qazi Amin in his work. See Edwards (2002).

[104] Nasrullah Mansur was the founder of the eponymous Mansur Network and an important commander in Paktia, Paktika and Khost during the Soviet-Afghan War. The Mansur Network is still active in Afghanistan. See Thomas Ruttig. "Loya Paktia's Insurgency: The Haqqani Network as an Autonomous Entity." In *Decoding the New Taliban*, by ed. Antonio Giustozzi, 57-88. (New York: Columbia University Press, 2009).

[105] Jalaluddin Haqqani is one of the most significant commanders of the entire Soviet-Afghan theater. He founded what would become the Haqqani Network, and was an important part of the Hizb-e Islami party that Yunus Khalis led.

[106] Mati'ullah Khan Wali Khel was one of the most important commanders in Khalis's party to never achieve fame in the West. He was in charge of the territory southwest of the Khost-Gardez Pass centered on Ziruk district, and commanded one of only a handful of permanent bases for Hizb-e Islami (Khalis) in Afghanistan.

[107] Din Muhammad has since held positions as the Governor of Nangarhar Province, the Governor of Kabul Province, and was recently nominated as the Minister of Border and Tribal Affairs. Dipali Mukhopadhyay's discussion of one of Din Muhammad's successors as governor of Nangarhar Province is revelatory. See Mukhopadhyay (2012). Her discussion of Gul Agha Sherzai is especially interesting because of the marked contrasts between him and Din Muhammad.

[108] Apparently he frequently had this hand axe with him. See Muhammad (2008), 45.

[109] Muhammad (2007), 34.

[110] Muhammad (2007), 33–35.

There are good reasons to be doubtful of this sort of hagiographical account; it appears designed to make Khalis look prescient in the face of the civil war of the 1990s.[111] True or not, the picture that Din Muhammad paints is clear and can be taken as representative of what a close confidante of Khalis thought about the mujahidin leadership in 1974. Din Muhammad claims that Khalis opposed the "wait and see" approach of many other mujahidin leaders and that he was suspicious of their unwillingness to directly address the leadership question.

The Failed Attempts to Unite the Mujahidin into One Political Party

Whatever Khalis's political approach might have been, he did not seek a leadership role in the evolving organizational infrastructure of the Afghan Islamist exiles.[112] Instead, he worked as the prayer leader (imam) in a mosque in the town of Bara.[113] Before long, he began teaching at the nearby Hadiqa al-'Ulum madrasa and prepared a series of lectures for the massive number of university students who were taking refuge in Pakistan. Khalis eventually collected these lectures for publication in his book *The Spirit of Islam*.[114] Although Khalis was definitely not politically inactive during this period, David Edwards is right to point out that he kept a low profile compared with the other major mujahidin leaders.[115]

There had long been tension between Burhanuddin Rabbani and Gulbuddin Hekmatyar, but the premature revolt in Afghanistan that Hekmatyar helped to plan in 1975 may have permanently soured his relationship with Rabbani and other mujahidin

---

[111] There are several important sources that were either unavailable as of writing, or were not able to be included in the analysis because of time constraints. In the future, it is hoped that a coordinated analysis of these sources can help to settle any outstanding questions of source bias in the biographical literature. The most significant known sources that were not included in this report are: Yunus Khalis's theoretical book *The Spirit of Islam*, which includes an extensive discussion of the pillars of Islam and the different types of jihad; Yunus Khalis's articles from the journals *The Beam of Light* and *The Message of Truth*, some of which are available from Princeton University's Firestone Library; Yunus Khalis's theological work *The Explanation of the Creed of al-Tahawiyah*; and the full text of Khalis's 1994 article on gender and politics entitled "Men and Women Are the Two Ministers (Pillars?) of Human Society."

[112] Such as they existed; it is not clear what form these groups took at this time.

[113] Muhammad (2007), 33.

[114] It is not known when this book was printed, although the Library of Congress stamp on the copy I reviewed would indicate that it was not printed after 1980. Ahmadzai describes the contents of the book as an exposition on the five types of jihad. See Ahmadzai, 83–84, and Muhammad (2007), 33.

[115] Edwards (2002), 247-248.

leaders.[116] It did not help that Hekmatyar, "almost alone among the party's student leaders,"[117] had chosen to remain in safety in Pakistan when the uprising took place. The rebellion may have resulted from an attempt by the hotheaded younger mujahidin of the Muslim Youth to sidestep their more cautious elders in the mujahidin (like Rabbani), but it ended in a near complete disaster that dealt a massive blow to the developing resistance movements. In the wake of this defeat, it became apparent to many people involved with the mujahidin leadership that serious action had to be taken to unify the various factions before a fight against the government in Kabul could take place.

In his book *Before Taliban*, David Edwards describes how Qazi Amin and others who were attempting to mediate between Hekmatyar and Rabbani came to Khalis to enlist his help in unifying the movement.[118] The ethnic and generational differences between the factions of Rabbani and Hekmatyar were increasingly significant, and it may not have been possible at that point to create a working union of their parties. In any event, Khalis was not interested. There may have been several attempts to recruit him to this cause, and Din Muhammad gives a unique perspective on this political jockeying in his biography of Khalis. In his version of events, Jamil al-Rahman, Mawlawi Ghulam Rabbani and Mawlawi Rahmat Khan came from Kunar Province, and Nasrullah Mansur and Jalaluddin Haqqani from Loya Paktia[119] to encourage Khalis to take charge of a new unified mujahidin political party that could heal the split between Burhanuddin Rabbani and Gulbuddin Hekmatyar.[120] Many of these men would eventually become his close associates and commanders, and Khalis gave the project serious consideration. According to Din Muhammad, Khalis spoke separately with both Hekmatyar and Rabbani, telling them that he would perform this duty as leader of a unity party only if they were willing to submit completely to his conditions. This was apparently unacceptable, and Khalis's name was withdrawn from consideration.

---

[116] Edwards (2002), 236.
[117] Edwards (2002), 236.
[118] Edwards (2002), 248.
[119] This means "Greater Paktia," and refers to the region of Paktia, Paktika and Khost. In U.S. military parlance it is often referred to as "P2K." It is a relatively distinct cultural region within Afghanistan and thus both U.S. officers and Afghans have need of geographical term referring to the area.
[120] Muhammad (2007), 35–36.

Events would unfold dramatically over the next three years with a succession of attempts to patch the growing rifts among the various factions of mujahidin. All would ultimately fail, but the way that they failed is instructive. The Islamist factions of Gulbuddin Hekmatyar and Burhanuddin Rabbani seem to have done the most damage to any prospects for a more permanent union of Sunni mujahidin. The animosity between these two leaders exerted a centrifugal force on the Islamist movement in Afghanistan that helped to overwhelm the repeated attempts to unify and then reunify the mujahidin. However, it seems clear in retrospect that Pakistan's willingness to spread funding across an increasing number of Sunni parties played an important role in fracturing the mujahidin. Forming a separate party allowed a faction to express important differences in ideology and to mobilize distinct affinity groups, but it also meant direct access to funding and war matériel from the Pakistani government. At a minimum, Pakistan's initial openness to funding new Sunni parties may have encouraged leaders like Sayyaf and Nabi Muhammadi to maintain control of their political organizations even after they failed in their original purpose of uniting the mujahidin in one camp.

Whatever the initial motivations may have been for forming different parties in the first years of the jihad, these splits allowed ethnic, generational, confessional and other affinity-group distinctions to increasingly characterize the mujahidin political parties. The clerical parties of Nabi Muhammadi and Yunus Khalis thus developed a somewhat distinct group of clients and commanders from the Sufi parties of Gailani and Mujaddidi or the Kabul Islamists like Hekmatyar and Rabbani.[121] But it was far from clear in the mid-1970s that this eventual articulation of party affiliation along clerical/Sufi/Kabul Islamist lines was inevitable. In fact, many governments and leaders expended enormous political capital in the 1970s to prevent precisely that kind of development.

In May 1976 Qazi Amin was named the leader of the new party that would supposedly unify the partisans of Hekmatyar and Rabbani.[122] Amin was well liked and, in the

---

[121] The heavy presence of private-madrasa-educated clerics and mullahs in the parties of Nabi Muhammadi and Yunus Khalis helps to explain why so many leaders from their parties eventually gained prominence in the Taliban movement.

[122] Muhammad (2007), 36; and Edwards (2002), 240. After the dissolution of the party that he initially headed in 1976, Qazi Amin would become an important leader in Hizb-e Islami (Gulbuddin).

words of David Edwards, he was viewed as a "fundamentally decent person."[123] The new unity party was named simply "the Islamic Party" (Hizb-e Islami), and the former political organizations were theoretically disbanded with its creation. Unfortunately, this did little to bridge the gaps among the various factions of mujahidin, and Qazi Amin was soon replaced as party head by Mawlawi Sakhidad Faiz.[124] Faiz fared no better, and he submitted his resignation after a week.

Whether because of outside pressure or their own determination, mujahidin efforts to unify the fractured movement continued even in the wreckage of the first Hizb-e Islami. After Faiz's resignation, Nasrullah Mansur, Hekmatyar and others went to Muhammad Nabi Muhammadi in the hope that he might be willing to lead a new unity party.[125] Nabi Muhammadi accepted, and "the Movement of the Islamic Revolution" (Harakat-e Inqilab-e Islami) was formed. It is important to note here that the first Hizb-e Islami party was formally dissolved with the creation of Harakat. Although Nabi Muhammadi and others appealed to Khalis directly to join Harakat, Khalis apparently had a low opinion of Nabi Muhammadi's leadership ability, and he never joined the new party.[126] Apparently, even some of those who joined Harakat soon had second thoughts.

Before long, the tentative alliance of Rabbani and Hekmatyar under Harakat-e Inqilab fell apart again when Rabbani took a trip to Saudi Arabia and created "the National Salvation Front" (Jebha-ye Nejat-e Milli) with Sibghatullah Mujaddidi.[127] Rabbani himself would soon abandon this Sufi party to resurrect the old Jami'at-e Islami. By this point, Yunus Khalis was probably already considering forming his own group, and the availability of the well-known Hizb-e Islami name must have made this option even more tempting. It seems that he expressed reservations about whether Harakat-e Inqilab could last much longer, and he disliked the political maneuvering that

---

[123] Edwards (2002), 241.

[124] Muhammad (2007), 36. Relatively little is known about Faiz and he only appears briefly in the Khalis biographies.

[125] Muhammad (2007), 37; and Edwards (2002), 244. Muhammad Nabi Muhammadi, like Yunus Khalis, was educated at Akora Khattak at the Dar al-'Ulum Haqqaniyya. It is not known when Nabi Muhammadi would have graduated, but since Nabi Muhammadi was born in 1937, he almost certainly went to Akora many years after the Dar al-'Ulum Haqqaniyya had been established.

[126] Edwards (2002), 248. Although the conversation took place much later, Khalis expressed his doubts to David Edwards by saying "I and some of my friends didn't accept him because he couldn't lead this union. He is a good scholar and can teach, but he can't do this work."

[127] Muhammad (2007), 37.

distracted the mujahidin from directly engaging the foe.[128] In theory, he could have thrown his support behind Hekmatyar, but David Edwards rightly points to Khalis's "resentment at being subordinate to younger and less experienced men."[129]

His exact motivations may never be clear, but at some point Khalis created his own Hizb-e Islami, and Hekmatyar eventually left Harakat and did the same.[130] These parties would become so radically different in structure and membership that it is hard to imagine that Khalis and Hekmatyar could ever have worked in the same chain of command, and it is little more than ironic that their parties bore the same names.

Surprisingly enough, even as all these leaders fled Harakat-e Inqilab, the party persisted. This could be because unlike Qazi Amin, Nabi Muhammadi was a practiced politician who longed for the advantages offered by a prominent leadership position. He had been a member of parliament and had famously come to blows with Babrak Karmal during a parliamentary session.[131] When Harakat began to hemorrhage support, Nabi Muhammadi simply reinvented it as his own political party instead of disbanding it. In the midst of this chaos, Sayyid Ahmed Gailani came to Peshawar and created what was to be the second Sufi party, and sixth party overall; "the National Front" (Mahaz-e Milli).[132]

The seventh and final official mujahidin party was the inadvertent result of a third attempt to unite the mujahidin under the banner of the "Islamic Union for the Liberation of Afghanistan" (Ittihad-e Islami Baraye Azadi-ye Afghanistan).[133] This time 'Abd al-Rab Rasul Sayyaf was chosen to lead the organization.[134] Like the first Hizb-e

---

[128] Muhammad (2008), 44.

[129] Edwards (2002), 249.

[130] Known as Hizb-e Islami (Khalis), and Hizb-e Islami (Gulbuddin).

[131] Edwards (2002), 244. Babrak Karmal was a well-known leftist politician and activist who eventually became chairman of the PDPA (People's Democratic Party of Afghanistan) and head of Afghanistan's communist regime between 1979 and 1986.

[132] Din Muhammad gives a concise account of the nearly simultaneous creation of these parties, albeit without much detail. See Muhammad (2007), 44–45.

[133] The name of this and the other parties is almost never given in the full form in the Persian or Pashto literature, and we follow that convention here by referring to the party simply as Ittihad-e Islami.

[134] Din Muhammad's account of how Sayyaf came to be the leader of Ittihad-e Islami is interesting. He claims that when the Russians invaded, Sayyaf was freed from prison and obtained a membership card in Hizb-e Islami (Khalis). He was then nominated by Khalis to be the leader of a new union of mujahidin

Islami and Harakat-e Inqilab before, Ittihad-e Islami failed to realize its lofty goals of binding the different mujahidin factions together in one political organization. If Sayyaf was disappointed he kept it to himself, and when Ittihad-e Islami ceased to function as a union, Sayyaf converted it into his own personal political party.

It is easy to imagine that these political parties coalesced relatively quickly once they were declared by their respective leaders, but the primary sources tell a more complex story. Urgent military necessity and the need to access money through official channels helped to crystallize the various parties to a certain degree. But whereas all of the parties would scramble to quickly achieve the proper status to secure international funding, it is not clear how quickly their structures evolved. As explored below, some of Khalis's earliest military forays into Afghanistan had a disorganized and almost desperate character because the system for distributing weapons and materiel in the late 1970s was in a state of flux. By contrast, Hekmatyar and Rabbani both represent a somewhat special case: they inherited a cadre of activists who were informed by their political awakening within the Kabul Islamist movement.

Hekmatyar quickly turned Hizb-e Islami into "a political party in the modern and specifically Leninist sense,"[135] and although Rabbani never created such a centralized organization, he benefited from the common political experience that many of his commanders shared with one another. However, it is less clear whether Sayyaf's organization ever had such cohesion,[136] and there is relatively little information about how effective the Sufi parties of Gailani and Mujaddidi were at transferring Sufi spiritual networks directly into a chain of command for the mujahidin. Lastly, Khalis apparently moved into Afghanistan to fight even before he formally declared the creation of his political party. Although the primary source accounts have a clear mythologizing element to their description of this first movement of Khalis's group into Afghanistan, the biographical narratives provide a unique window into this little-understood time.

---

which became the Ittihad-e Islami. When it failed, he kept its name for his own party, and the rest is history. See Muhammad (2007), 39–40.

[135] Edwards (2002), 276.

[136] Roy seems to argue that Sayyaf's Ittihad-e Islami barely functioned as a party at all; Sayyaf gave many weapons to small and isolated groups with no overall political control or agenda, nor any meaningful links between them. See Roy, 135–136.

Khalis's Attempts to Cultivate Jihad, and the First Days of his Political Party

Before the seven official Sunni parties had taken shape, a large meeting of elders took place near Peshawar. Khalis met with this group of supporters of the jihad, the majority of whom were Nangarharis like him.[137] According to Din Muhammad, these were Khalis's words to the group:

> The active jihad must begin. Within two days I am departing for Nangarhar, and everyone who is prepared to fulfill the duty of jihad may accompany me.[138]

In Din Muhammad's account, the members of the assembly seemed to think that Khalis was joking and laughed at him as they responded, "You don't have any weapons or ammunition."[139] Khalis failed utterly to gain support at this gathering, but he left for Nangarhar anyway. Din Muhammad claims: "I was the only person present from this meeting who went together with him to Nangarhar; we did not wait for weapons and ammunition."[140] True or not, this does not seem like the expected mythology of an organization on the verge of becoming one of the premier military forces of the frontier war.

These sources would have us believe that it was far from a foregone conclusion that Khalis's group would become a powerful political and military force. In fact, rather than claim that the group was well equipped and supported, Din Muhammad states that their first mission against the government in Kabul was an attack on a local telephone line executed with the small ax that Khalis carried.[141] After this, Din Muhammad says they came to an agreement with Jamil al-Rahman, Jalaluddin Haqqani and Mati'ullah Khan to begin an "active" jihad together,[142] and to name their group

---

[137] Muhammad (2008), 44.

[138] Muhammad (2008), 44–45.

[139] Muhammad (2008), 44.

[140] Muhammad (2008), 45.

[141] Muhammad (2008), 45.

[142] The use of this term "active jihad" is frequent in Din Muhammad's account, and it seems to reflect the fact that Yunus Khalis desired to come directly to grips with the Soviet foe even as his fellow leaders spent most of their time in Peshawar. Khalis's eagerness to be on the front line of the conflict is well known. Even Peter Tomsen, who is evidently not a fan of Khalis, remarks on this: "Khalis's preference for

Hizb-e Islami.[143] Apparently, the creation of this party was not the result of Khalis's own political maneuvering, nor was it the direct descendant of an older formal organization like the Muslim Youth or one of the other Kabul Islamist groups. According to the biographical sources, Hizb-e Islami (Khalis) came about because a small group of leaders in adjacent provinces wanted to band together to fight. Khalis was far older and better known than the other men, and he may have become their leader simply by default.[144] The ethnic divisions that took place in the mujahidin movement relatively early in the 1970s were largely entrenched by the time that Khalis had risen to a position of prominence, and his party was almost entirely made up of eastern Pashtuns.

The effect of reading Din Muhammad's version in tandem with Ahmadzai's account of the same events is to underscore how dangerous and tentative Khalis's initial days in Afghanistan actually were. Insofar as there is a mythic component to these accounts, it is located in the authors' depiction of the precarious early state of the jihad. According to Ahmadzai, when Khalis went into Nangarhar Province in 1979, he brought only seventy men, twenty weapons, and twenty-seven blankets.[145] This was scarcely enough equipment to defend them from government attacks and to keep away frostbite, much less for conducting offensive operations. When Khalis's group moved into the Luy Wali Valley after running out of ammunition, food had become so scarce that "a boiled egg

---

the war zone distinguished him from the other Peshawar party leaders. Gailani, Rabbani, Nabi, and Mojaddedi rarely entered Afghanistan. Sayyaf's and Hekmatyar's trips into Afghanistan were brief, heavily guarded, well photographed, and usually just over the border to ISI-supplied base camps. Khalis was different. He buckled on his pistol and joined operations against the enemy in the Tora Bora area of southern Nangarhar, sleeping under the stars and firing at regime outposts." See Tomsen, 306.

[143] Muhammad (2008), 45. It is worth noting that there is exceedingly little good information about Jamil al-Rahman in the available literature. Although Din Muhammad claims that Jamil al-Rahman was one of the original commanders involved in the creation of Hizb-e Islami (Khalis), in a recent interview Habib al-Rahman vigorously denied this. Habib al-Rahman is a former mujahidin commander from Kunar who joined Jamil al-Rahman's Jama'at al-Da'wa political party after the end of the Soviet Afghan War. See al-Rahman (2013). Clearly, much more research is needed before we can say anything conclusive about Jamil al-Rahman's politics in the early 1980s.

[144] With this said, Khalis also had a longstanding connection to the aristocratic Arsala family of Nangarhar and the three Arsala brothers were some of his most important supporters ('Abd al-Haq, 'Abd al-Qadir and Haji Din Muhammad). In addition, Jalaluddin Haqqani was an alumnus of the Dar al-'Ulum Haqqaniyya, and it is probable that this shared connection to Mawlana 'Abd al-Haq Haqqani factored into the connection between the two men.

[145] Ahmadzai, 33.

28

was shared between three men."[146] Instead of offering to help, the local people sent a letter threatening the mujahidin with war if they did not decamp.[147] This may help to explain why the Nangarhari elders had laughed at Khalis when he invited them to join his jihad a few days before.

Beyond a doubt, these narratives were designed to underscore the toughness and endurance of the early fighters, and in this goal Din Muhammad and Ahmadzai succeeded. But they also give us a window into the earliest stages of the jihad, when matériel and funding were not yet readily available from the Pakistani government. In this context, the assets that mujahidin were able to seize from government forces were critical. The only reason that Khalis entered Nangarhar with military equipment at all was because Jalaluddin Haqqani and Mati'ullah Khan had raided a depot in Ziruk District the year before.[148]

Rather than operating as the independent commander of his own jihadi force, Khalis comes across in these early narratives as a poorly equipped leader of a medium-sized element who had to depend on his connections with a handful of important people to survive. At this point in the fight Hizb-e Islami (Khalis) did not yet effectively exist, and Khalis's seventy fighters were little more than a local nuisance to the authorities in Nangarhar. Over the course of a few weeks however, Khalis was able to draw volunteers to his camp from all over Nangarhar,[149] and what began as discrete localized rebellions eventually joined together to span the most important provinces in the eastern Afghan frontier.

But before that could happen, Khalis needed effective support. Only when a major group of already important commanders chose him as their leader did his "active jihad" become anything more than a rhetorical device. The course of history is often unpredictable, and some of the people connected to Khalis such as Jalaluddin Haqqani and Usama bin Ladin were destined to become many times more famous than Yunus Khalis himself. We will now turn to the relationships that Khalis developed with these

---

[146] Ahmadzai, 37. Interestingly enough, this valley is in the same district where Khalis would soon build the famous Tora Bora base with the cooperation of local villagers.
[147] Ahmadzai, 37.
[148] Ahmadzai, 33–34.
[149] Ahmadzai, 39.

men, some of whom are among the best known and most controversial jihadi leaders of the age.

Evaluating Yunus Khalis's Personal Ties to Bin Ladin and Mullah Omar

The Mythos of Yunus Khalis and Bin Ladin

In the 1990s, interest in Yunus Khalis was largely confined to his role as a leader in the Soviet-Afghan War.[150] That changed when the 9/11 attacks dramatically increased international interest in Usama bin Ladin and the history of al-Qa`ida. Suddenly Khalis's relatively peripheral relationship with Bin Ladin was deemed newsworthy.[151] In fact, however, very little direct contact between these two men is visible in the primary sources.[152] We can state with some confidence that Khalis hosted the al-Qa`ida leader at the housing development near Jalalabad known as Najm al-Jihad.[153] There is also little question that later in the same year Bin Ladin took control of Khalis's old mujahidin base at Tora Bora.[154] But in spite of the relative clarity on these two points,

---

[150] There are many good books that discuss Khalis in this context. Some historically minded examples of works from the 1990s are: Aleksandr Lyakhovsky. *The Tragedy and Heroism of the Afghan War.* (Moscow: GPI Iskona, 1995); Roy (1990); Rubin (2002); and Asta Olesen. *Islam and Politics in Afghanistan.* (Richmond: Curzon, 1995). Jere Van Dyk's book *In Afghanistan* gives a more thorough discussion of Khalis's personality and commanders than most journalistic works, and it also bears rereading. See Jere Van Dyk. *In Afghanistan.* (NYC: Coward McGann, 1983).

[151] This is not to say that *all* books published since 2001 discuss Khalis in the context of al-Qa`ida. David Edwards' book *Before Taliban* is excellent and does not try to tell a story of Khalis's supposed connections to Usama bin Ladin. With that said, most of the works which mention Khalis since 2001 discuss his role in the context of al-Qa`ida and President George W. Bush's "War on Terror," and leave little space for commentary about his role in the Soviet-Afghan War.

[152] The two most important points of contact between Khalis and Bin Ladin in the known primary sources are related to two events. The first of these was Khalis's attempt to arrange a negotiation between Usama bin Ladin and the Saudi government. See Talai, 95–96. The second event was the well-known period of time when Bin Ladin stayed at Yunus Khalis's housing development at Najm al-Jihad in 1996. See Muhammad (2007), 202–204. 'Abd al-Kabir Talai states clearly that Usama bin Ladin arrived, probably in Peshawar, to meet the various leaders of the mujahidin political parties at some point after "the jihad was already going along in a successful manner." See Talai, 93–94. While this is vague, Talai seems to mean that Bin Ladin did not meet Khalis in the early days of the jihad. Talai goes on to say that "Bin Ladin in this initial period did not have relations with Khalis that are very worth remembering." See Talai, 94. Although Khalis and Bin Ladin probably met before 1996 there is no primary source information which states when or where this might have taken place. This is the reason for the heavy focus on Khalis's contact with Usama bin Ladin in 1996; there is little evidence for their interactions at any other time.

[153] See Muhammad (2007), 202; Bergen, 159; Scheuer (2006), 164–165; Scheuer (2011), 105–106; Tomsen, 543, 608; Rubin, xxvii; Wright, 255; Coll, 327; Weaver (2005); Peters 2009, 8.

[154] See Scheuer, 2011, 106, 131; Tomsen, 250; Wright, 259–260; Brown and Rassler, 105–106; Weaver (2005); Omar bin Laden, 175. Haji Din Muhammad is unclear on this point and says only that it is possible that Usama bin Ladin was at Tora Bora in 2001. See Muhammad (2007), 128.

the conclusions that can be drawn about Khalis's relationship with Bin Ladin based on these interactions in 1996 are far from obvious.

In the absence of more easily accessible information about al-Qaʿida's activities in Nangarhar, Khalis's role as a host attracts much attention. It is difficult to evaluate assertions about the critical importance of Usama bin Ladin's relationship with Yunus Khalis, but two recently released interviews from sources close to Bin Ladin and the wealth of material in the Khalis biographies add important new layers to our understanding of the surprising connections between the relative calm in parts of eastern Afghanistan in the 1990s and the spread of al-Qaʿida to those regions.[155] The results tend to de-emphasize the operational importance of Yunus Khalis as an al-Qaʿida facilitator while dramatically underlining the significance of provincial-level commanders to the growth of Bin Ladin's organization in 1996.

Unfortunately, the provincial level leaders such as Engineer Mahmud and Haji Saz Nur who figure prominently in numerous primary sources[156] about al-Qaʿida in Nangarhar are still relatively poorly studied in the West. Their obscurity may help to explain the proliferation of a set of historical traditions linking Bin Ladin's arrival in Jalalabad and the expansion of his organization in Afghanistan to his relationship with the well-known mujahidin leader Yunus Khalis. The first step in this analysis will be to examine the most commonly cited components of the received wisdom about Yunus Khalis's connections to Usama bin Ladin and, by extension, to Mullah Omar.

In general, these historical traditions focus on the arrival of the al-Qaʿida leadership in Nangarhar in 1996, and the organization's eventual establishment of relations with the

---

[155] The two new al-Qaʿida sources are the recently released transcript of an Ayman al-Zawahiri interview, and the text of Anand Gopal's interview with Sheikh Muhammad Omar ʿAbd al-Rahman. See al-Zawahiri (2012), and Muhammad (2012). The two most important Khalis biographies are Muhammad (2007); and Ahmadzai. Nangyal's brief work on Khalis and the excerpt from Khalis's autobiography are also of related interest, even though they mostly deal with theoretical political issues. See Nangyal 1989, 146–159.

[156] See Muhammad (2007), 202; Omar bin Laden, 149–153; Wahid Muzhda. *Afghanistan During the Five Years of Taliban Rule.* (Tehran: Nashreney, 2003), 31; Wahid Muzhda. "8 AM Afghanistan (8 Subh)." *How Did Bin Ladin Return to Afghanistan?* (October 16, 2012). http://www.8am.af/index.php?option=com_content&view=article&id=28004:1391-07-24-15-22-22&catid=3:2008-10-31-09-37-07&Itemid=554; Linschoten and Kuehn, 135; Bergen, 158. Abu Jandal writing in this last Bergen citation names only Engineer Mahmud as central to the arrival of Bin Ladin.

Taliban. In the absence of more information about the variety of connections that Bin Ladin maintained with provincial leaders in the province, most authors tend to cite Khalis as the critical figure who provided Usama bin Ladin with a place to stay at Najm al-Jihad in 1996, when Khartoum ejected al-Qa`ida under pressure from the United States.[157] This tradition is based in fact, but it tells us little about Khalis's actual connection to al-Qa`ida and obscures the significant role played by provincial commanders in bringing Bin Ladin to Nangarhar. Additionally, given the cultural context of eastern Afghanistan, Yunus Khalis's willingness to act as a host can be read as little more than a fulfillment of his tribal obligations as a good Pashtun to provide housing to a friend in need.

Many also add that the al-Qa`ida leader took over Khalis's old base complex at Tora Bora soon after his arrival in Jalalabad,[158] but this assertion is of even less analytical value than the above since it is not clear whether Tora Bora was in use at this time or if Khalis had anything to do with the transfer of the base to Bin Ladin's control. The al-Qa`ida leader's decision to live at Tora Bora in the fall of 1996 says more about his personal desire for seclusion than it does about his relationship with Yunus Khalis. At most, knowledge of Bin Ladin's movement to Khalis's old base in 1996 can help explain why the al-Qa`ida leadership fled to Tora Bora during the NATO invasion of Afghanistan in 2001.

In addition to making general claims about Yunus Khalis's involvement with the arrival of the al-Qa`ida leadership in Jalalabad in 1996, some authors seek to establish a deep personal connection between Khalis and Usama bin Ladin. A few go so far as to say that

---

[157] See Bergen 2006, 159; Scheuer (2006), 164–165; Scheuer (2011), 105–106; Tomsen, 543, 608; Rubin, xxvii; Wright, 255; Coll, 327; Weaver (2005); and Gretchen Peters. "How Opium Profits the Taliban." (Washington, D.C.: U.S. Institute of Peace, 2009), 8. I use the proper name Najm al-Jihad here in order to be as specific as possible, even though many of these sources do not specify Najm al-Jihad as the location at which Khalis hosted Usama bin Ladin. Bin Ladin probably stayed at several locations in Jalalabad, but he eventually came to Khalis's neighborhood in Najm al-Jihad.

[158] Michael Scheuer asserts the importance of Tora Bora to Usama bin Ladin during the Soviet-Afghan War and after his return to stay with Khalis in 1996. For this general claim see Scheuer (2011), 106, 131. Tomsen's work also heavily emphasizes the importance of Tora Bora to Usama bin Ladin's experience in the Soviet-Afghan War; see Tomsen (2011). See also Wright, 259–260; and Weaver (2005). Weaver actually claims that Khalis transferred the caves to Bin Ladin: "Khalis gave him [Usama bin Ladin] two of his fighting positions in the mountains—Tora Bora and Milawa." Brown and Rassler are nearer the mark when they claim that the Eastern Shura (they use the term "Jalalabad Shura," but it is the same body) gave Bin Ladin permission to use Tora Bora. See Brown and Rassler, 105–106.

Khalis acted as a father figure to Bin Ladin,[159] and there are periodic assertions in the secondary literature that Khalis and/or his son Anwar al-Haq Mujahid helped Bin Ladin escape from Tora Bora in 2001.[160] As previously mentioned, Talai's 2012 biography of Khalis is the only primary source to confirm that Usama bin Ladin referred to Khalis as "the Father Sheikh," but there are numerous examples of Afghans referring to Yunus Khalis as "Papa Khalis" in the Pashto sources.[161] Leaving aside any questions this may raise about how unique or important Bin Ladin's choice of nickname for Khalis may have been, Bin Ladin's use of this term of endearment seems to have been rooted in Khalis's willingness to accept him as a friend even after the international community had turned against al-Qa'ida.[162] Affection and reverence notwithstanding, this personal relationship certainly does not seem to have guaranteed that Khalis and Bin Ladin saw eye to eye politically.[163]

The final major component of these historical traditions in the secondary literature involves Yunus Khalis's alleged role in connecting Usama bin Ladin with Mullah Omar. Many Western authors claim that the Taliban leader was a member of Hizb-e Islami (Khalis) during the Soviet-Afghan War[164] and, more important, that Khalis introduced Bin Ladin to Mullah Omar in 1996 or 1997.[165] It may be true that Mullah Omar fought under Hizb-e Islami (Khalis) at some point in the 1980s, but he almost certainly had no

---

[159] Weaver (2005). In this article, Weaver cites an interview with Scheuer, which is by Dressler and Jan. See Dressler and Jan, 4. See also Jere Van Dyk's comments on this point in Van Dyk (2006). Van Dyk admits his uncertainty, but he does not give a clue about his source.

[160] Tomsen, 608. Weaver cites Michael Scheuer on this point for her article. See Weaver (2005). Van Dyk does not claim that Khalis directly aided in Bin Ladin's escape but instead claims that his sons did. See Van Dyk (2006). Phillip Smucker is also a major proponent of this idea and summed up his theory about Khalis and Anwar al-Haq Mujahid's involvement in Bin Ladin's escape in an article written about the trial against a former Khalis commander who later died in Guantanamo. See Smucker (2009).

[161] In fact, this is precisely how he referred to in the titles of two of his biographies: *Khalis Baba [papa, father or grandfather] upon the Road to Eternity*, and *Khalis Baba Step by Step*. Baba is a relatively flexible word and can refer to either a father or a grandfather. See Ahmadzai (2006); and Talai (2012). It is entirely possible, even likely, that Bin Ladin's nickname for Khalis ("the Father Sheikh") was an extension of the same kind of affection demonstrated for the old man by his own commanders and friends. In that sense, there may be very little remarkable about the appellation.

[162] Talai, 96.

[163] Muhammad (2007), 202–204; and Talai, 93–97.

[164] Weaver again cites Scheuer in Weaver (2005). See also Coll, 288; Van Dyk (2006); Lynch, 23; Scheuer (2006), 165.

[165] The source for this information in Weaver, and by extension Dressler, et al., appears to be Scheuer. See Weaver (2005); Dressler and Jan, 4; Van Dyk (2006).

direct contact with Yunus Khalis during the jihad. And significantly, no solid evidence that Yunus Khalis had a role in introducing Usama bin Ladin to the Taliban leader yet exists. In sum, these historical traditions in the secondary sources seek to give Yunus Khalis a critical role in both the "return" of al-Qa'ida to Afghanistan and the highly charged, albeit widely misrepresented, interactions between al-Qa'ida and the Taliban.

We can confirm that Yunus Khalis helped to host Usama bin Ladin for a brief period in 1996, that Bin Ladin moved some of his followers to Tora Bora soon after his arrival in Jalalabad and that Mullah Omar had some level of involvement with Hizb-e Islami (Khalis) during the Soviet-Afghan War. However, even though these particular elements of the Khalis-tradition are true, there is still great uncertainty about the overall analytical value of the broader historical mythos of Yunus Khalis. Unfortunately, the almost unqualified reiteration of both the true and the tendentious portions of the Khalis tradition has obscured the complexity of his politics and the identities of the actors who *were* actually closely involved in the development and growth of al-Qa'ida.[166] This leads in turn to a consistently warped account of Khalis's activities after the Soviet-Afghan War and serves to put him in a kind of mythical "quaternion of jihad" together with Mullah Omar, Usama bin Ladin and Jalaluddin Haqqani.

---

[166] There is no reason to draw the conclusion that Khalis was a father figure to Bin Ladin in anything other than name based on the currently available evidence. Furthermore, there are too many different accounts of how Bin Ladin escaped from Tora Bora for us to evaluate any assertions about Khalis's or his son's involvement. It is possible, even likely, that either Khalis or his son *hoped* that Bin Ladin would escape from Tora Bora, but there is no real evidence that either of them did anything to help make this happen. Smucker claims that Anwar al-Haq Mujahid was "at Bin Laden's side when he and his hard core fighters decided to withdraw from Jalalabad to Tora Bora," but this tells us nothing about how Bin Ladin escaped from the mountain base. See Smucker (2009). Alex Linschoten and Felix Kuehn claim that Mullah Omar fought under the Hizb-e Islami (Khalis) commander 'Abd al-Raziq in Kandahar, but they also point out that Mullah Omar switched parties more than once during the jihad. See Linschoten and Kuehn, 477, 479. This is the most robust assertion made to date about Mullah Omar's involvement with Hizb-e Islami (Khalis), and it may indeed be true. Even so, this is no reason to draw the conclusion, as some authors do, that these two men were close or had a working relationship prior to the arrival of the Taliban in Nangarhar in 1996. Lower-level leaders tended to show more loyalty to field commanders than to party leadership, and these field commanders switched parties so frequently that it is barely even relevant that a young Mullah Omar may have been involved in Hizb-e Islami (Khalis) at some point. It is also worth mentioning that Kandahar was a relatively low priority for Hizb-e Islami (Khalis). Even Khalis's most important Kandahar commander during the war, Mullah Malang, makes almost no appearance in the Khalis biographies. Mullah Malang was a significant figure in Kandahar, but he maintained relatively loose ties with Peshawar and was minimally involved in the politics of the party. Finally, Sheikh Muhammad's interview with Anand Gopal seems to suggest that Khalis had no role in introducing the al-Qa'ida leader to Mullah Omar. See Muhammad (2012).

Khalis's Relationship with Bin Ladin: a Number of Views

Such a distortion of Khalis's historical role invites scholars and analysts to make bold assumptions about his connections to the Taliban movement and his support for Bin Ladin's increasingly violent post-1996 agenda. Unfortunately, assumptions like this fly directly in the face of the (admittedly scant) available evidence.[167] This confusion about the nature of Yunus Khalis's connections and politics might be of relatively minor concern if its effect were confined to investigations of him and his political party. However, our understanding of Khalis has consequences for larger issues such as the current reconciliation efforts in Afghanistan that hope to convince certain insurgent groups to permanently renounce their ties to al-Qa`ida.

Thomas Lynch suggests that the personal relationships between top leaders like Khalis, Bin Ladin and Jalaluddin Haqqani are the most important points of connection among their respective jihadi organizations. This leads him to conclude that the death of Yunus Khalis in 2006 and Usama bin Ladin in 2011 might unravel the relationship between al-Qa`ida and certain jihadi organizations active in eastern Afghanistan.[168] But it is not clear that these personal relationships between Bin Ladin and top Afghan leaders constitute the best way to analyze the inter-organizational dynamics of the Afghan mujahidin and al-Qa`ida. And even if they were, one should remember that al-Qa`ida was not significantly deterred when several of their most important Afghan operational

---

[167] Khalis was apparently not a fan of Mullah Omar's Kandahari brand of conservative politics. See Muhammad (2007), 105–107. In addition, the only evidence that we have of Khalis's opinion about Usama bin Ladin's call to internationalize the jihad indicates that he argued against Bin Ladin's 1996 declaration calling for jihad against the American presence in Saudi Arabia. See Muhammad (2007), 203–204. He apparently viewed Bin Ladin's break with Saudi Arabia as lamentable, and nowhere do we see evidence that Khalis agreed with al-Qa`ida's aggressive stance against the Saudi kingdom or the United States. Instead the primary sources tell us that Khalis attempted to reconcile Bin Ladin with the Saudi government; and apparently even in 1996, when the al-Qa`ida leader was staying in Najm al-Jihad, Khalis seemed to believe that a rapprochement was still possible. See Talai, 95–96; and Muhammad (2007), 202–203. Khalis's declaration of jihad against the NATO forces in 2003 must be viewed as an entirely different kind of political act than Bin Ladin's aggression against the United States in the late 1990s.

[168] Lynch, 10. Lynch's footnotes on Khalis are especially revelatory and clearly point to the emphasis he places on Khalis's connection to Mullah Omar and Usama bin Ladin in his arguments about jihadi organizations in eastern Afghanistan. See footnote 42, Lynch, 23.

facilitators were killed in late 1996.[169] The reality is that there is still a lack of clarity regarding who Usama bin Ladin's most important contacts in Afghanistan were. However, the prevalence of information about the operational connections between al-Qa`ida and Jalaluddin Haqqani,[170] Engineer Mahmud[171] and Haji Saz Nur[172] suggests that these men were demonstrably far more significant to the development of Usama bin Ladin's organization than "the Father Sheikh" Yunus Khalis.

In a bizarre twist, the secondary material written in English about Khalis and Bin Ladin gives a much more detailed and enthusiastic account of their relationship than the material produced by al-Qa`ida or Hizb-e Islami (Khalis). The al-Qa`ida leader Ayman al-Zawahiri stated in a recently taped interview that "the most striking aspect of this relationship was that Shaykh Yunus Khalis harbored Shaykh Usama Bin Ladin in Jalalabad when the Sudanese Government, may it get what it deserves from God, ejected him."[173] Al-Zawahiri makes no argument that Khalis acted as a mentor to the former al-Qa`ida leader and never mentions Mullah Omar. Instead he expresses his surprise and approval at Khalis's willingness to host Bin Ladin in a time of need. While not too much should be made of what is absent from al-Zawahiri's interview, his special emphasis on Khalis as a host matches up well with other sources. In all likelihood, this willingness to invite Bin Ladin into his home during a difficult time was what inspired the affection that Talai claims the al-Qa`ida leader felt for Khalis.

---

[169] Both Engineer Mahmud and Haji Saz Nur were killed in an ambush in the fall of 1996 in strange circumstances. See the narrative in Muhammad (2007), 98–99. According to Wahid Muzhda, these two men "were killed in revenge for the blood of Shemali Khan by the hand of his brother." See Muzhda (2012). This version of events is basically confirmed by Omar bin Ladin, who does not mention the name of Shemali Khan, but reports that "the killers were the bandit's brother and other members of the family. This was the bandit put to death last year by Mullah Nourallah [Haji Saz Nur]." See Omar bin Laden, 216.
[170] See Brown and Rassler, 75–76. Their discussion of the early development of training and operational connections between Haqqani's group and the nascent al-Qa`ida is revelatory.
[171] For more information on Engineer Mahmud's connections to Usama bin Ladin's arrival in Afghanistan, see Muhammad (2007), 202; (source: Abu Jandal) Bergen, 158; Muzhda (2003), 31; (source: Abu al-Walid al-Masri) Linschoten and Kuehn, 135; and Roy Gutman. *How We Missed the Story: Osama bin Laden, the Taliban, and the Hikacking of Afghanistan.* (Washington, DC: United States Institute of Peace Press, 2008), 89–90.
[172] For more information about Haji Saz Nur's connections to al-Qa`ida arrival in Afghanistan in 1996, see Muhammad (2007), 202; Muzhda (2003), 31; Muzhda (2012); Omar bin Laden, 150; (source: Abu al-Walid al-Masri) Linschoten and Kuehn, 135; Muhammad (2012); and Gutman, 89–90.
[173] Ayman al-Zawahiri, interview by unknown. *al-Sahab.* Translated by Combating Terrorism Center. (2012).

Din Muhammad, who was recently nominated as the minister of tribal and border affairs by the government in Kabul, has a clear personal stake in downplaying Yunus Khalis's connection to Bin Ladin. So it is doubly intriguing that Din Muhammad's account agrees very closely with al-Zawahiri's, both in the discussion of Bin Ladin's stay with Khalis and in Khalis's response to criticism over his decision to host the al-Qa'ida leader.[174] These and other available primary sources never purport that the two men had a mentor-pupil relationship. Instead they make relatively modest claims that Khalis helped to provide Bin Ladin with a place to stay in spite of his infamy,[175] and they suggest that Khalis urged the al-Qa'ida leader not to declare jihad against Saudi Arabia.[176] The two men were doubtless acquainted with one another, and according to Bin Ladin's son Omar, they enjoyed reminiscing together in Jalalabad in 1996.[177] However, there is nothing in the available texts to suggest that this amicable relationship was operationally critical to al-Qa'ida, much less that Yunus Khalis became the principal al-Qa'ida facilitator in Nangarhar when Bin Ladin arrived in 1996.

Of course, not everyone agrees with the interpretation that Khalis and Bin Ladin were little more than old jihadi acquaintances from the days of the Soviet-Afghan War. The best known evidence in favor of a claim that the two had a particularly close relationship comes from a brief citation from a book written by Abu Musab al-Suri, a strategist and trainer who consulted on behalf of al-Qa'ida:

---

[174] Al-Zawahiri says that when the Saudi Ambassador to Pakistan told Khalis that Bin Ladin was dangerous, Khalis responded: "My brother, if cattle from the Land of the Two Holy Mosques [Saudi Arabia] came to me I would have sheltered them, so how can I not shelter the mujahidin?" See al-Zawahiri (2012). Although it is not clear who is speaking with Khalis in Din Muhammad's account, the sentiment is similar: "Some people told Mawlawi Khalis that Usama bin Ladin is angry with the Saudi government, and that if he stays in your town [Najm al-Jihad] then may it not happen that the Saudi government should become angry with you. Mawlawi Khalis said: 'If Usama bin Ladin had permission to do jihad in Afghanistan, well why should we deny him the ability to live here now? Once he is reconciled with his country, then he will go back.'" See Muhammad (2007), 202–203.

[175] Muhammad (2007), 202–203; al-Zawahiri (2012); Abu Jandal (2005). It is worth noting that both Din Muhammad and al-Zawahiri may be exaggerating Khalis's response to criticism about harboring Bin Ladin in order to make him seem like an exceptionally good host.

[176] Talai, 95–96; and Muhammad (2007), 203–204. This section of Din Muhammad is ostensibly about Khalis's response to Bin Ladin's request for legal opinions about the permissibility of declaring jihad in Saudi Arabia. According to Din Muhammad, and there is no evidence to the contrary, Khalis's response was a strong negative, and Bin Ladin published his declaration of jihad anyway.

[177] Omar bin Laden, 154–155.

I heard something incredible from Yunis Khales ... during a meeting [...] He said to Abu Abdallah [Bin Ladin], in his thickly accented but proficient Arabic, "I have nothing but myself, and it is very dear to me. However, you are more precious to me, and your well-being is more important than my own. You are our guest, and no one can get to you. If anything happens with the Taleban, tell me. Though there is little I can do after they reach you, I will do all I can."[178]

At first glance this text can be seen as proof that Yunus Khalis was making an extraordinary offer of protection to Usama bin Ladin, which might support an assertion that the relationship between the two men was close enough to extend into ideological or operational cooperation. However, cultural and historical clues about the context of the conversation and signals in Khalis's wording argue against such a clear-cut interpretation.

The Context of Bin Ladin's Stay with Khalis in 1996

When the aforementioned conversation occurred, Bin Ladin had recently arrived in Nangarhar as an exile from Sudan. It is worth asking at the outset why he chose Jalalabad as his safe haven instead of returning to the camps al-Qa`ida maintained near Jalaluddin Haqqani's Zhawara facility in Khost Province.[179] The most likely answer is that by the time Bin Ladin was under pressure to flee Sudan, Haqqani's territory in Paktia and Khost had come under Taliban control.[180] Since the al-Qa`ida leader was initially uncertain whether the Taliban were friends or foes,[181] he chose to relocate to Nangarhar where his contacts were still operating outside the Taliban's authority. However, Nangarhar would not remain outside the Taliban's reach much longer.

Although Khalis apparently extended his aegis to Bin Ladin in the above quotation by al-Suri, Khalis also stated that "there is little I can do after they reach you."[182] By 1996 it is questionable whether Khalis was in a position to defend the al-Qa`ida leader against

---

[178] Scheuer (2011), 106.
[179] Brown and Rassler (2012).
[180] The Taliban took Loya Paktia in early 1995, over a year before Bin Ladin left Sudan for Jalalabad.
[181] Omar bin Laden, 159; Linschoten and Kuehn, 139–140; Brown and Rassler, 101.
[182] Scheuer (2011), 106.

the Taliban with a military force. In that context, Khalis's parting words to Bin Ladin[183] may have referred more to a possible diplomatic intercession than to an armed intervention. According to al-Suri, Yunus Khalis wanted to reassure the al-Qa`ida leader by stating his good intentions, but Khalis also deftly signaled that Bin Ladin needed to manage his expectations for what could be done if he was ever captured by the Taliban.

Khalis's recognition of his limited influence was rooted in recent experience. Not long before this 1996 discussion with Bin Ladin, Yunus Khalis had been powerless to prevent the Taliban from abusing the brother of a close friend in Paktika,[184] and he would continue to have a troubled relationship with the Taliban in the coming years. Rather than being taken literally, this text should be seen as a tactful expression by Khalis of his desire to help a guest even as he frankly admits that his real capacity to offer assistance is limited. In addition, most accounts of the cultural norms of Pashtunwali emphasize the importance of *melmastia* (hospitality) for the reputation of a host in a community.[185] The available evidence indicates that Khalis genuinely cared about traditional aspects of Pashtun culture such as melmastia,[186] and in this context Khalis's offer of protection to Bin Ladin was actually rather unremarkable. The unique political environment of Nangarhar in early 1996 was probably a far more important element in Bin Ladin's decision to come to Jalalabad than his friendship with Yunus Khalis.

---

[183] As transmitted by al-Suri: "I will do all I can." See Scheuer (2011), 106.

[184] The story of how the Taliban dealt with Mati'ullah Khan's brother and his depots in Ziruk is revelatory and is only one in a string of vignettes that Din Muhammad uses to mark the lack of trust between Khalis's people and the Taliban. Khalis attempted to intercede on behalf of Mati'ullah Khan's brother Haji Sarfaraz, and the Taliban assured him that Sarfaraz and the Ziruk base were in no danger. But even as negotiations between Sarfaraz's people and the Taliban were taking place, the Taliban attacked the Ziruk depots, and Sarfaraz was forced to flee with his family to Waziristan. See Muhammad (2007), 87–88. The exact extent of Khalis's friendship with Mati'ullah Khan is not known, but Din Muhammad clearly presents the relationship between the two men as close.

[185] An extensive discussion of Pashtunwali is outside of the scope of this report, but in general it is viewed as a set of traditions that shape expectations of what will be considered good manners and good behavior by members of a Pashtun community. One of the most important components of this is *melmastia* (hospitality). Hospitality in this context has both a social and a political function.

[186] Din Muhammad discusses Khalis's reputation as a good friend and a fine host extensively. See especially Muhammad (2007), 227–229.

Many Western works on al-Qa`ida explicitly set out the goal of understanding Usama bin Ladin's relationship with Nangarhar Province through Tora Bora and Jalalabad.[187] It is widely known that Bin Ladin stayed near Jalalabad with Khalis, but there is continuing uncertainty about the specific circumstances of his arrival.[188] Similarly, the narrative that Usama bin Ladin escaped from Tora Bora in December 2001 drives many authors to investigate his connection to that famous Nangarhari mujahidin base. Yet there is surprisingly little *factual* information about Tora Bora available to Western readers.[189] While the Khalis biographies do not definitively settle these questions, they do provide critical background details about politics in Nangarhar and the histories of Tora Bora and the Najm al-Jihad housing development, where Khalis played host to Bin Ladin and many others. Understanding these contextual clues is the first step toward demystifying the complex intersection of Hizb-e Islami (Khalis), the Taliban, the Eastern Shura[190] and al-Qa`ida in the 1990s.

Khalis's "Retirement" in Nangarhar

Of course, some of the most important contextual clues for an analysis of Khalis and his role in Nangarhari politics during this period have little to do with famous bases and housing schemes. The biographies remind us that Khalis was a frail man of seventy-six years of age when Bin Ladin arrived in Jalalabad. His health was failing so badly that he

---

[187] Weaver's 2005 article "Lost at Tora Bora" is only one of the more obvious examples. See Weaver (2005).

[188] Linschoten and Kuehn, 134–136. The authors do a good job of citing a variety of sources and giving some sense of the confusion around the historical issues related to Bin Ladin's arrival in Jalalabad.

[189] There were a number of completely fictitious accounts of the legendary "Bin Ladin Ant Farm" written in late 2001, some of which eventually generated complex graphic representations and maps. For a brief description of this media feeding frenzy with the attending gross lies and exaggerations, see Edward Jay Epstein. "Fictoid #3: The Lair of bin Laden." *Netherworld.* (Date unknown). http://www.edwardjayepstein.com/nether_fictoid3.htm. Although it is nearly impossible to evaluate Omar Bin Ladin's discussion of Tora Bora without more sources, he brings up a number of new points about how his family came to occupy the base. See Omar bin Laden (2009).

[190] The Eastern Shura is sometimes referred to as the "Jalalabad Shura" or the "Nangarhar Shura." This shura was led by Din Muhammad's brother Haji 'Abd al-Qadir. It was a multilateral shura including all of the mujahidin parties with a presence in Nangarhar, and it was based in Jalalabad. Din Muhammad credits this body with preventing the Afghan Civil War from spreading into Nangarhar. It is worth noting that although 'Abd al-Qadir had been a major Khalis commander during the Soviet-Afghan War, he does not appear to have been acting under Khalis's direction as the leader of the shura. Khalis's control over 'Abd al-Qadir and other powerful commanders had significantly diminished by the time that the Eastern Shura was created.

was nearing the end of his working life,[191] and his political party had already effectively disintegrated.[192] Even in the earlier 1990s, Khalis had almost no direct hand in national or provincial governance during the Afghan Civil War.[193] In fact, Khalis seems to have had only a peripheral connection to his own erstwhile subordinate commanders and allies in the late 1990s, let alone to organizations like al-Qaʿida. According to the biographies, Khalis's chief role in the mid- to late 1990s seems to have been as a negotiator and adviser to other (younger) political actors, and even this did not guarantee him a sympathetic audience. Engineer Mahmud, who had been one of

[191] Although the sources make some effort to say that Khalis was still able to accept visitors even when he was sick, there is ample evidence that by 1998 he was already in rapid decline. Michael Semple reports that in 2002 Khalis was bedridden and communicated only through a son. Additionally, Semple explains that a former student of Khalis (Fidai) claims that Khalis was in a similar state of ill health since at least 1998; Semple (2012). This is generally confirmed by Jere Van Dyk's somewhat later account of visiting Yunus Khalis after 2001. See Van Dyk (2006). For the biographical information about Khalis's health, see Ahmadzai, 49–51; Din Muhammad (2007), 105. Din Muhammad describes a meeting between Mullah Muhammad Rabbani, Nabi Muhammadi and Khalis that took place in 1995 or earlier. Already by this point Khalis's health was bad enough that he preferred to have other people speak on his behalf at the gathering. Khalis only spoke after he decided that he was displeased with what Nabi Muhammadi was telling the Taliban.

[192] There is occasional reference to the party existing well beyond the early 1990s, but once the National Commander's Shura formed in 1990, Khalis's most important commanders began to strike out on their own. In fact, Jalaluddin Haqqani was an important driving force behind the effort to set up the commander's shura and hosted one of the meetings at his base in Zhawara. See Tomsen, 402. Khalis still exercised a great deal of influence in his role as an adviser to some of these commanders, but not all of them listened and after the war he was no longer able to compel them to do so. Additionally, it is not clear what kind of relationship Khalis had with Jamil al-Rahman at the beginning of the jihad, but by the 1990s Khalis had long since lost influence with him and other Salafi-oriented Kunar mujahidin leaders. Jamil al-Rahman created his own Wahhabi state in Kunar Province in spite of Khalis's vociferous objections to the elections held there. See Pakistan Times. "Afghan Mujahideen Hold Elections in Kunar." In *Afghanistan Forum 18, 1990*, by Afghanistan Forum, 14. New York, 1990. Ruttig argues that the Hizb-e Islami (Khalis) continued to exist into the post-Taliban era and that it split into a pro-government and an anti-government faction led by Khalis's son Anwar al-Haq Mujahid. See Ruttig, 22. It does appear that certain groups affiliated with Khalis continued to operate under the name of his faction of the old Hizb-e Islami-ye Afghanistan, but it is less clear whether these were really organizations in the institutional sense of Khalis's old political party or what conclusions we should draw on this basis about the continuation of Khalis's party into the post-Soviet era.

[193] "He did not have an individual share in the government positions of the mujahidin government of Afghanistan…" See Ahmadzai, 49. It is true that he briefly held a few different positions in the national government as a member of the Afghan Interim Government after 1989, but he became progressively less involved throughout most of the 1990s. His main role seems to have been limited to offering advice, as we see on Muhammad (2007), 109–110. Khalis did hold a position as the Minister of the Interior for the Afghan Interim Government (AIG) for some time, but after the beginning of the Afghan Civil War, the AIG's ability to control the course of events rapidly declined and Khalis does not appear to have been closely involved in other mujahidin governments after he left the AIG.

Khalis's most important commanders and remained a supporter of Usama bin Ladin, openly flouted Khalis's advice to exercise caution as the Taliban arrived in Nangarhar in late 1996.[194] But there may be more to Khalis's disengagement from a direct leadership role in national politics than his age, ill-health and external political factors.

It is suggestive that after the fall of Najibullah's regime in Kabul in 1992, Yunus Khalis shifted his attention away from national politics toward more local and pietistic pursuits. His activities at Najm al-Jihad were closely connected with the history of the famous Mullah of Hadda through more than just the choice of a name for the neighborhood. In fact, Khalis's new housing development, which was theoretically built in part to provide housing to the destitute, was situated immediately west of the area where the Mullah of Hadda was known to host hundreds of people, including both Sufi adepts and the poor of Nangarhar.[195] Khalis's activities in this period could be characterized in many different ways based on the scant available sources, but there is little to suggest that he was an active participant in organizations like al-Qa`ida or even the Eastern Shura in Jalalabad. It seems clear that many recent books rely too heavily on Khalis to help explain the Nangarhar element in the growth of al-Qa`ida. However, other historical problems could be much more fruitfully approached through an investigation of Khalis's political influence on eastern Afghanistan.

In the 1990s, the power struggles among regional political elites in Afghanistan resulted in very different responses to the factional violence of the civil war, and, later, to the rise of the Taliban. After the Soviet-Afghan War ended, there was a kind of transition of control in Nangarhar from the hands of Dr. Najibullah's government to the Eastern Shura led by 'Abd al-Qadir.[196] The Eastern Shura was the main player in Nangarhar politics in the chaotic period between the fall of the Najibullah government in 1992 and the Taliban takeover of the province in September 1996. Although Khalis was not an active member of this body, Din Muhammad argues that he had a clear vision for the

---

[194] Muhammad (2007), 97. According to Din Muhammad, Engineer Mahmud was ultimately killed in an ambush partly because of his disregard for Khalis's warning.

[195] For more information about the Mullah of Hadda, also known as Najm al-Din Akhundzada, see David Edwards. *Heroes of the Age: Moral Fault Lines on the Afghan Frontier.* (Berkeley: University of California Press, 1996).

[196] 'Abd al-Qadir was eventually chosen as the vice president of Afghanistan by Hamid Karzai and served in this office and as minister of public works until he was assassinated in 2002.

Eastern Shura's role in keeping Nangarhar out of the civil war.[197] As Khalis's health and influence steadily declined, he continued to interfere episodically at critical points in national politics.[198] But in spite of these high-profile engagements, Khalis gradually became more involved in local concerns. We will begin our analysis of his connection to various major jihadi leaders by evaluating the histories of the two most important locations of his influence on Nangarhari politics: his base at Tora Bora and his housing development at Najm al-Jihad.

Tora Bora, and the Importance of Zhawara to the Birth of al-Qa`ida

The Tora Bora base in Pachir aw Agam District was the third Nangarhari base occupied by Hizb-e Islami (Khalis) in the late 1970s.[199] The organization hurriedly abandoned the first fortification when ammunition and supplies ran out in the face of a major government attack,[200] and when its members moved to a new location in Luy Wali, the locals tried to eject them from the valley.[201] They overcame these tensions, and the Luy Wali base became known for its strong defenses, but it was so snowy there in the winter and so difficult to reach by foot that the mujahidin immediately began searching for a

---

[197] See Muhammad (2007), 89–90. On page 89, Khalis says, "My role and the Eastern Shura's role must be to make peace between the warring parties …"

[198] The three most potentially significant of these interventions involved attempting to prevent the spread or continuation of the violent struggle for power over the countryside. First, when the Taliban had approached Paktia, Din Muhammad claims that Jalaluddin Haqqani sought Khalis's advice about what to do with the Taliban forces on his doorstep. Allegedly, Khalis told Haqqani to reach an agreement with them and avoid fighting. See Muhammad (2007), 86. Later, when the Taliban negotiated with the Eastern Shura to organize a combined attack on Kabul, Khalis intervened to prevent the shura from participating in such a venture and averted the assault on the capital. See Muhammad (2007), 89–90. Finally, after 1996 Khalis traveled to Kandahar specifically to gain an audience with Mullah Omar and to convince the Taliban leader to come to a peace agreement with the Northern Alliance. See Muhammad (2007), 109–110. It is unfortunate that all of these sources are from Din Muhammad since they may be thus subject to his confirmation bias in favor of Yunus Khalis. Over time, however, more sources likely will be found, or else evidence may be uncovered to explain why only Din Muhammad mentions these episodes.

[199] The story is not continuous but the construction of these bases is described in Ahmadzai, 34–41. It is worth mentioning that Ahmadzai places the declaration of a new party by Khalis at some point after his initial movement into Nangarhar. This is especially interesting because Khalis's group was so woefully ill-supplied at that early stage. Khalis had already begun coordinating with Jalaluddin Haqqani and Mati'ullah Khan by the mid-1970s, but it is not as clear when his relationships with other leaders began or when his established connections became more operationally focused.

[200] Ahmadzai, 36.

[201] Ahmadzai, 37.

new position.[202] They found an ideal spot at a small village of the Suleiman Khel tribe in an area near Spin Ghar[203] called Tora Bora. After consultation with Khalis, the locals decided that their homes "would be given out of their own free taste and satisfaction as a charitable trust [waqf] to the jihad for the sake of God."[204] Apparently, they voluntarily moved out of the area, and in 1979 their village became the mujahidin base of Tora Bora.[205]

Tora Bora may have achieved great fame through its connection to Usama bin Ladin from 1996 to 2001, but it was neither the only permanent base built by Hizb-e Islami (Khalis) on Afghan soil during the war nor was it closely tied to the development of al-Qa'ida in the late 1980s. Khalis's party maintained three other major bases in Afghanistan throughout the jihad: Jalaluddin Haqqani's Zhawara base, Mati'ullah Khan's Ziruk base and a base near Nazyan district of Nangarhar Province.[206] Little is known about the significance of the Ziruk and Nazyan fortifications.[207] On the other hand, Zhawara has since become famous[208] as one of the most important logistical hubs of the entire resistance effort in eastern Afghanistan.[209] Ironically, when the Soviets

---

[202] Ahmadzai, 40–41.

[203] It is worth noting that Spin Ghar is the Pashto name for both a particular mountain peak and the area around it. The name translates as "White Mountain," and it is occasionally referred to by that name in English or by the Persian equivalent "Kuh-e Safid."

[204] Ahmadzai, 41.

[205] Din Muhammad gives a briefer version but still corroborates the location of Tora Bora at Suleiman Khel in Agam (Pachir and Agam form one district), and gives the same date for the construction of the base in 1979. See Muhammad (2007), 41. Interestingly, he claims that the first Hizb-e Islami (Khalis) base was in a little-known area of Khost Province and states that while Haqqani and Mati'ullah Khan built the base, Khalis sent 'Abd al-Qadir, 'Abd al-Haq, 'Abd al-Wahhab and Mawlawi Najm al-Din to work there before the Tora Bora base was constructed.

[206] Muhammad (2007), 261. Anticipating the likely questions that readers might have about permanent bases in Afghanistan during the war, Din Muhammad mentions that there were very serious dangers of aerial bombardment, and that this limited the number of permanent Hizb-e Islami (Khalis) bases in Afghan territory to four.

[207] There is much more written about the Ziruk base in "Mawlawi Khalis's Life, Art, and Thought." This base was in the area directly south of the Khost-Gardez Pass in Paktia Province, and was assaulted by the Taliban early in their push into Loya Paktia. See Muhammad (2007), 87.

[208] It has generated a great deal of commentary, including short pieces in Russian about the base and the battle to overtake it in 1986. For an interesting example, see the article "Dzhavara" by Victor Kutsenko; Victor Kutsenko. "Dzhavara." (*Literaturnaya Rossiya*. 2001 1-June). http://www.litrossia.ru/archive/42/soul/988.php.

[209] David Edwards reports that by the time that he visited Zhawara in 1984, the base had already become a key hub in the route for mujahidin transiting to locations further afield in Afghanistan. Interestingly, he

made a massive push to overwhelm Zhawara in 1986, they set in motion a sequence of events that helped give rise to a new Arab mujahidin movement separate from 'Abdullah 'Azzam's long-established Maktab al-Khidamat.[210]

The Zhawara battle in 1986 was one of the largest of the entire Soviet-Afghan War. The combined Soviet and Democratic Republic of Afghanistan forces succeeded in collapsing the cave where Jalaluddin Haqqani was taking cover, and the communists even pushed the mujahidin out of Zhawara for several hours at the height of the fighting.[211] Haqqani was forced to issue a call for help at the beginning of the long battle, and large numbers of mujahidin were mobilized in response. Many fighters arrived to assist in the defense of Zhawara, possibly including Arabs of the Maktab al-Khidamat, who had not frequently been involved in frontline fighting up to that point.[212] In fact, when Yunus Khalis arrived in Miranshah to help coordinate the defense, he sat together with a group of Arab mujahidin in Haqqani's home to listen to news of Zhawara on the radio.[213]

The complex story of the Arab presence at the Battle of Zhawara has yet to be fully uncovered, and Vahid Brown cites Arab sources that both downplay and laud Maktab al-Khidamat's involvement in the fighting.[214] Clearly some of the Arabs were more

---

also noted that there were large numbers of "mujahidin" at the base who were either captured Afghan Army soldiers or deserters. See David Edwards, interview by Kevin Bell. *Unpublished Interview with David Edwards* (2012 11-December). Brown cites a source claiming that a huge percentage of the supplies and materiel shipped to the mujahidin went through Haqqani's base at Zhawara. See Brown and Rassler, 68.

[210] The Maktab al-Khidamat, or the Maktab Khidamat al-Mujahidin al-'Arab, was an organization set up to coordinate the Arab volunteers who arrived in Pakistan hoping to help with the jihad. 'Abdullah 'Azzam was the leader of this movement and is often described as being opposed to Bin Ladin's goal of setting up a separate Arab fighting force.

[211] According to Brown and Rassler, Haqqani was actually rescued by a man who would later become a founding member of al-Qa`ida. See Brown and Rassler, 72.

[212] Din Muhammad's biography of Khalis makes it clear that there were Arabs present at Jalaluddin Haqqani's home during the Battle of Zhawara. He does not expand on the purpose behind their presence, but it is likely that they were connected either to Haqqani's ongoing efforts to integrate Arabs into the jihad, or to the older Maktab al-Khidamat organization headed by 'Abdullah Azzam. See Muhammad (2007), 207–208. For more information on the Arab mujahidin involvement in this battle, see Brown and Rassler, 71–74.

[213] Muhammad (2007), 207. This is not to say that the atmosphere was particularly brotherly. One of the more foolish Arabs made an attempt to abominate the practice of listening to music while Khalis was there. The ensuing argument as recounted by Din Muhammad makes for amusing reading.

[214] Brown and Rassler, 73–74.

satisfied with the experience than others were, and the battle appears to mark a split in the Arab mujahidin community of Maktab al-Khidamat. Some of the Arabs continued to follow 'Abdullah 'Azzam's policy of assisting the Afghan mujahidin parties relatively indirectly, while others followed Usama bin Ladin and helped him create his newly dubbed base "Ma'sadat al-Ansar" near Jaji in October 1986.[215] The Ma'sada base was to become one of the centers of a new kind of Arab mujahidin force designed to fight on the front lines, and it soon gained a nickname that must have seemed prosaic at the time: "al-Qa'ida al-'Askariyya" (the Military Base).[216]

Ma'sada's logistical and operational ties to Haqqani's base at Zhawara were deep. Brown and Rassler describe an interlocking network of preparatory training and leadership cadre that was shared between the proto-al-Qa'ida organization and Haqqani's forces beginning in the late 1980s. They argue that "to join the nascent al-Qa'ida ... meant first training with the Haqqani network."[217] Tora Bora was much closer to Bin Ladin's base than Zhawara was, but there is currently no evidence that Khalis or Tora Bora played any direct role whatsoever in the early development of Bin Ladin's new organization, and Talai directly denies that Khalis had any significant relationship with Bin Ladin during the Soviet-Afghan War.[218] Khalis granted a large degree of operational autonomy to major commanders such as Haqqani and 'Abd al-Haq, and generally did not centralize decision making in his party.[219] Therefore, although Haqqani probably informed Khalis of some of his plans, it cannot be assumed that Haqqani was acting under direct orders to foster a strong relationship with Arab mujahidin such as Bin Ladin.[220]

---

[215] Brown and Rassler, 75. This is seen as a major departure from 'Abdullah 'Azzam's policy because the purpose of this new base was not to provide support to the Afghan mujahidin but instead to create a separate and primarily Arab fighting force with its own priorities and operations.

[216] The name of the base may be directly related to the naming of the organization, but the creation of the base should not be directly construed as the beginning of the al-Qa'ida organization as such. This base was constructed in 1986, but it is believed that al-Qa'ida itself was not actually declared as a new organization until late 1988 as the Soviets were withdrawing from Afghanistan. See Bergen 2006, 75.

[217] Brown and Rassler, 75.

[218] Talai, 94.

[219] Edwards's comparison of the different leadership cultures of the parties is revelatory. See Edwards (2002), 251–252, 274–275.

[220] The most that can be said about Khalis's direct involvement in the increasingly international focus of al-Qa'ida and the Haqqani Network is that Khalis evidently wrote a letter in support of a jihad in southern Sudan in 1991. This was recovered when Enaam Arnaout's computer was seized in Sarajevo. See Brown and Rassler, 80.

Haqqani had obvious financial reasons for building his own patronage and support networks and appears to have worked diligently to find links to the Persian Gulf.[221] However, Haqqani was also engaged in the fabulously profitable business of collecting and selling scrap metal gleaned from abandoned materiel after the end of the Soviet-Afghan War. In fact, he became so well known for this trade that one of his most famous nicknames in eastern Afghanistan is still "Haqqani Kabarri" (Haqqani the Junkman). This scrap-metal business helped give Haqqani the financial wherewithal to remain largely independent from Khalis and other national leaders during the turbulent early 1990s. So, while it is clear that Jalaluddin Haqqani had a strong relationship with Yunus Khalis, there is no reason to believe that Haqqani's activities at Zhawara were being controlled or funded by Khalis.

There are abundant sources attesting to Bin Ladin's connections to Zhawara and other bases in Khost during the 1980s, but nothing available from this period suggests that the al-Qa`ida leader had significant operational ties to Tora Bora.[222] That only changed when Bin Ladin fled from Sudan to Jalalabad in 1996. In fact, Anand Gopal's interview with Sheikh Muhammad suggests that Bin Ladin's first meeting with a representative of the Taliban took place at Tora Bora.[223] This is supported by Omar Bin Ladin's brief account of his father's first meeting with a Taliban messenger.[224] However, few clues exist about how or even if Tora Bora was being used from the fall of Najibullah's government in 1992 until Bin Ladin's arrival in 1996. Based on what is known of Khalis's political activities during this time period, land management at Tora Bora seems unlikely to have been a pressing priority for the Hizb-e Islami leader.

---

[221] Although not enough research has been publicly presented on this topic, in 2002 authorities seized a computer belonging to Enaam Arnaout in the office of the "Benevolence International Foundation" which detailed some of the financial activities of a charity that funded both al-Qa`ida and Haqqani bases. See Brown and Rassler, 90–91. Significant portions of the court documents related to this case are available publicly from the Department of Justice.

[222] It is true that some Arab fighters participated in the Battle of Jalalabad, but this took place in mid-1989 and does little to establish the importance of Tora Bora to al-Qa`ida or other Arab mujahidin groups.

[223] Muhammad (2012).

[224] Omar bin Laden, 175.

Khalis and the Afghan Civil War

For part of the early 1990s Yunus Khalis was still an active national-level political figure in Afghanistan. He was the interior minister in the Afghan Interim Government, and he even threatened to run for leadership of the country in opposition to Sayyid Ahmed Gailani at one point.[225] However, according to Din Muhammad, Khalis spent much of his diminishing political capital in the 1990s by trying to convince Rabbani, Hekmatyar and others to stop fighting one another.[226] One cannot naively ascribe an unassailable moral authority to Yunus Khalis on this basis,[227] but discussions of his actions during the civil war are notably absent from most Western accounts of the period. In Din Muhammad's view, Khalis eventually became convinced that the mujahidin government was part of the problem, and he counseled his commanders not to take the official positions they were offered.[228]

Unfortunately, while Din Muhammad gives us some idea of Khalis's activities after he "returned" to Nangarhar in 1994,[229] there is very little in the biographies to tell us about Khalis's activities in Peshawar during this period. This is unfortunate, in part because it is known that around 1992 Usama bin Ladin was working from Peshawar to mediate between the belligerent parties in Afghanistan,[230] and it is unlikely that Khalis was unaware of these efforts. Other than Talai's description of Khalis's attempts to mediate between the Saudi government and Bin Ladin, little is known about Khalis's activities

---

[225] Muhammad (2007), 70. His publicly stated reason for objecting to Gailani's candidacy was that Gailani's father was from Iraq, and therefore Gailani was not really an Afghan. There is no way of knowing what his real reasoning was, but this seems like the kind of political comment meant mostly for public consumption.

[226] Muhammad (2007), 62–63.

[227] Some authors grant a hallowed status to Afghan leaders of this period, and the objectivity of their work suffers for it. The pervasive assumption about 'Abd al-Haq's moral superiority because of his nonparticipation in the civil war is one of the chief problems with Lucy Morgan Edwards's otherwise fascinating book. See Lucy Morgan Edwards. *The Afghan Solution: The Inside Story of Abdul Haq, the CIA and How Western Hubris Lost Afghanistan.* (London: Pluto Press, 2011).

[228] Muhammad (2007), 64.

[229] Yunus Khalis spent a great deal of time traveling throughout the early and mid-1990s. Even after 1994, when he supposedly settled at Najm al-Jihad, he appears to have gone frequently to Peshawar. His move to Jalalabad in 1994 is marked as a permanent return mostly because that was when he built a new home for himself and broke ground on his new neighborhood.

[230] See the discussion of mediation in Brown and Rassler, 89–90.

during this period,[231] but there are isolated clues that might prove to be fruitful ground for future investigations. If nothing else, it must be noted that in 1991 both Yunus Khalis and Jalaluddin Haqqani penned statements of support for a jihad in Sudan,[232] not long before many of Bin Ladin's followers would move to Khartoum. Even though this certainly raises questions about why there is so little information in the biographies about Khalis's activities in Peshawar in the early 1990s, the letter has no direct bearing on the broader primary source narrative that Khalis was not involved in the civil war.

In fact, to the extent that Din Muhammad's biography of Khalis makes a consistent argument, it is that Khalis was not one of the culpable parties in the devastating violence of the Afghan Civil War.[233] Although this should not be blindly accepted, Din Muhammad makes several thought-provoking points about Khalis's involvement in a kind of "Nangarhari exceptionalism" that helped to keep the civil war out of the province.[234] This discussion of regional politics is less obscure than it may seem at first blush. Although it is too early to state this claim definitively, the unique political situation in Nangarhar in the 1990s likely had a direct bearing on Bin Ladin's decision to seek refuge there.

---

[231] Talai, 95–96.

[232] Brown and Rassler, 90–91.

[233] There are numerous anecdotes that the author uses to demonstrate that Khalis worked to negotiate a settlement to the violence or told his commanders not to fight with other parties. For example, Din Muhammad recounts that in the mid-1990s when Khalis's bases came under fire by Hekmatyar's forces, Khalis told his commanders to retreat and abandon their posts rather than fight Hekmatyar. See Muhammad (2007), 88–89. However, the clearest example of Din Muhammad's attempt to paint a clear teleological story is when he prefigures the civil war in Khalis's first discussions with the mujahidin leadership in Peshawar. At one of the first meetings Khalis berated the mujahidin for not having a specific plan about who would take the leadership of the government when they came into power. Then when the civil war begins much later, Din Muhammad remarks that "And then that saying of Mawlawi Khalis's became true that 'one day the government will be entrusted to you, and you will not have made preparations or found a unified leadership.'" See Muhammad (2007), 34–35, and 58.

[234] Din Muhammad does not go into the economic incentives to maintain peace in the bustling Khyber Pass, but he extensively discusses the Eastern Shura. He goes so far as to credit the organization directly for preventing the outbreak of civil war in Nangarhar at one point. See Muhammad (2007), 263. The most specific words about Nangarhari exceptionalism are cited in reference to Khalis's attempt to convince the Eastern Shura *not* to participate in a Taliban plan to attack Kabul in 1996. Here Khalis is seen reminding the shura what it is that makes Nangarhar special and why their duty is to keep the peace. See Muhammad (2007), 90.

Given Din Muhammad's obvious pro-Khalis bias, the continued search for evidence that offers a different interpretation of Khalis's activities in this period is essential. For better or worse, however, all of the currently available evidence indicates that Khalis and his commanders went out of their way to avoid direct involvement in the Afghan Civil War.[235] This was not a guarantee that they shunned their contacts with al-Qa`ida and other foreign terrorist groups however, and so the next stage in this analysis will examine the details about Usama bin Ladin's arrival in Jalalabad in 1996.

Usama bin Ladin's Arrival in Nangarhar in 1996

Bin Ladin's arrival in Nangarhar in 1996 is a difficult puzzle to unravel. The movement was intended to be secret,[236] and there are still many open questions about the chain of events that led him to Jalalabad. Various authors note the comments made about Bin Ladin's movement to Afghanistan by valuable sources like Wahid Muzhda,[237] Abu Musab al-Suri,[238] Abu al-Walid al-Masri,[239] and Abu Jandal.[240] These are excellent

---

[235] Usama bin Ladin claimed in a book written about the 1987 Battle of Jaji that Khalis's lack of involvement in the civil war was admirable. See Scheuer (2011), 105. Omar Bin Ladin states that when a peace deal was reached to end the war, Khalis "threw his hands in the air and said that was it! He was finished with fighting." See Omar bin Laden, 154. Several works also discuss the decision of various Hezb-e Islami (Khalis) commanders not to participate in the civil war. See especially the discussion of Jalaluddin Haqqani's role as a mediator throughout Brown and Rassler (2012). Lucy Morgan Edward's book about 'Abd al-Haq is a semi-hagiographical work written from the starting premise that 'Abd al-Haq, a major Khalis commander, was not involved in the violence of the Afghan Civil War. See Edwards (2011). Khalis opposed the elections held by his erstwhile Kunar-ally Jamil al-Rahman. Jamil al-Rahman had ceased fighting actively for any of the mujahidin parties in 1984, and by the 1990s he was largely focused on his home region in Kunar; he seemed to have little interest in the contest for Kabul. And finally, Din Muhammad claims that the Eastern Shura led by his brother 'Abd al-Qadir was primarily responsible for preventing the spread of the civil war to Nangarhar. Although Din Muhammad is obviously painting a favorable picture of the shura and his brother's involvement, his overall interpretation about the importance of the multilateral shura led by his brother may be correct. See Muhammad (2007), 263.

[236] Muzhda's describes the elaborate layers of security and secrecy involved in the movement. See Muzhda (2003), 31. Bergen also cites a similar thought not identical version of Muzhda's story. See Bergen 2006, 158.

[237] Wahid Muzhda was an official in the Taliban Foreign Ministry, and may have worked for 'Abdullah 'Azzam in the 1980s. He wrote an interesting book entitled *Afghanistan Under Five Years of Taliban Rule*. See Muzhda (2003).

[238] Abu Musab al-Suri is a well-known jihadi thinker and trainer who eventually became involved with Bin Ladin's organization. He has written several books about the jihadi movement in Afghanistan and elsewhere. See Abu Musab al-Suri. "Afghanistan, the Taliban and the Battle for Islam Today." (*Combating Terrorism Center at West Point.* date of upload unknown). http://www.ctc.usma.edu/posts/afghanistan-the-

sources, but they tend to discuss different aspects of the story. This diverging focus has made it difficult to piece together the chain of events and the actors who were involved in Bin Ladin's move from Sudan. It is known that Sudan was under enormous pressure from the United States to expel the al-Qa`ida leader in the mid-1990s,[241] and when Khartoum ultimately yielded to Washington's wishes, Bin Ladin had few options for relocation. A much clearer picture of this chaotic time emerges by including in our analysis Anand Gopal's recent interview with Sheikh Muhammad,[242] and Din Muhammad's account of Bin Ladin's exile from Sudan in his biography of Khalis.[243]

In analyzing all of the available sources simultaneously, three people immediately stand out: the Hizb-e Islami (Khalis) commander Engineer Mahmud,[244] the Ittihad-e Islami commander Haji Saz Nur,[245] and the Hizb-e Islami (Gulbuddin) commander Fazl al-Haq Mujahid.[246] These are the individuals most frequently cited together in the primary sources for involvement in bringing Bin Ladin to Jalalabad. They flew to Sudan early in 1996, possibly under the invitation of the government in Khartoum to attend a

---

taliban-and-the-battle-for-islam-today-english-language; and Scheuer (2011), 106. Linschoten and Felix also discuss Scheuer's source. See Linschoten and Kuehn, 135.

[239] Ibid.

[240] Bergen, 158. Abu Jandal was Usama bin Ladin's bodyguard for several years.

[241] See The 9-11 Commission. "The 9-11 Commission." (*The 9-11 Commission Report.* 2004), 109–110.

[242] Muhammad (2012).

[243] Muhammad (2007), 202–204. Oddly enough Puhnamal Ahmadzai, who is openly supportive of the anti-NATO and anti-Karzai insurgency, never once mentions Usama bin Ladin in his biography of Khalis. This does not necessarily mean much, however, since Ahmadzai skips much of the 1990s in his biographical account.

[244] He was a Nangarhar-based commander of Hizb-e Islami (Khalis). He was apparently a bit of a hothead and ignored Khalis's advice not to contest control of the city as the Taliban marched toward Jalalabad. See Muhammad (2007), 97. Peter Tomsen also cites reports that Engineer Mahmud sold several prisoners to Arab fighters during the Soviet-Afghan war. The Arab fighters, he claims, then executed the prisoners brutally. See Tomsen, 306. For the primary sources that mention Engineer Mahmud in connection with Usama bin Ladin's arrival in Nangarhar, see Muhammad (2007), 202; Abu Jandal in Bergen 2006, 158; Muzhda (2003), 31; Muzhda (2012); Abu al-Walid al-Masri in Linschoten and Kuehn, 135.

[245] Haji Saz Nur was a major commander with Sayyaf's party. Din Muhammad describes him as the leader of Sayyaf's mujahidin in Nangarhar. For the primary sources that mention Haji Saz Nur in connection with Usama bin Ladin's arrival in Nangarhar, see Muhammad (2007), 202; Muzhda (2003), 31; Muzhda (2012); Omar bin Laden, 150; Linschoten and Kuehn, 135; Muhammad (2012).

[246] Fazl al-Haq Mujahid was an important leader of Hizb-e Islami (Gulbuddin) in Nangarhar. For the primary sources that discuss Fazl al-Haq Mujahid in reference to Usama bin Ladin's arrival in Nangarhar, see Muhammad (2007), 202; Muzhda (2003), 31; Muzhda (2012); and Muhammad 2012. In Gopal's interview with Sheikh Muhammad Omar 'Abd al-Rahman, Fazl al-Haq Mujahid is referred to as "Mujahid Saheb," and he is described as a representative of the Jalalabad Shura.

celebration of Sudanese independence, and presented the overtures that eventually convinced Bin Ladin to come to Jalalabad later that year.[247] Sources offer different suggestions about who met Bin Ladin when he arrived in Nangarhar, but these same three commanders are consistently associated with the al-Qaʿida leader's arrival and initial stay in Jalalabad.[248]

Evidence strongly suggests that these three were directly involved in bringing Bin Ladin to Nangarhar, but it is not known to what degree they acted on their own initiative in this undertaking. It is tempting to conclude that this group, made up of one commander from each of the three main parties in Nangarhar, may have been sent by the multilateral Eastern Shura. It would not necessarily have contradicted the Eastern Shura's anti–civil war politics to invite Bin Ladin to their province, and Gopal's interview with Sheikh Muhammad seems to suggest that the shura was involved.[249] Din

---

[247] Muhammad (2007), 202; Muzhda (2003), 31; Muzhda (2012); and Gutman, 89–90. Wahid Muzhda suggests that this delegation invited Usama bin Ladin back to Afghanistan to help them negotiate a peace deal with the strengthening Taliban movement. See Muzhda (2012).

[248] In one source, Wahid Muzhda is vague about who met Bin Ladin at the airport but clear about who kept tabs on him after arrival: "At Jalalabad, Usama came under the protection of the three commanders and Maulana Khales." See Muzhda (2003), 31. However, in a much more recent article that Muzhda penned in response to a work by Amrullah Saleh about Bin Ladin's arrival in Afghanistan, Muzhda states that 'Abd al-Rab Rasul Sayyaf, Sadiq Chakri, Danishyar, Fazl al-Haq Mujahid and Haji Saz Nur met Usama bin Ladin at the airport with a group of others. Muzhda adds that the group then ate lunch at Saz Nur's home. See Muzhda (2012). Abu Jandal mentions Engineer Mahmud greeting Bin Ladin upon arrival and then says that the al-Qaʿida leader was taken to be received at Yunus Khalis's home. See Bergen, 158. Abu al-Walid al-Masri claims that Engineer Mahmud, Saz Nur, 'Abd al-Haq and a Dr. Amin were on the tarmac the day Bin Ladin arrived. See Linschoten and Kuehn, 135. Al-Suri has little to say about Bin Ladin's actual arrival, but he discusses his reception at Khalis's home. See Scheuer (2011), 106. In another work al-Suri seems to mention a similar reception, but he does not give Khalis a prominent role in the anecdote. Instead, he simply says that Khalis's party had played a role in protecting the Afghan Arabs up to that point. See al-Suri, 37. Din Muhammad discusses the travel of these three commanders to Sudan but is silent about who meets Bin Ladin in Jalalabad. Sheikh Muhammad claims that Saz Nur and a "Mujahid Saheb" met their group when the plane landed. Anand Gopal confirms that this "Mujahid Saheb" is Fazl al-Haq Mujahid. See Muhammad (2012). Uniquely among sources with possible firsthand knowledge of the events of 1996, Camille Tawil claims that Khalis and Jalaluddin Haqqani also met Bin Ladin at the airport. See Camille Tawil. *Brothers in Arms: The Story of al-Qaʿida and the Arab Jihadists.* (London: Saqi Books, 2010), 147. This cannot be disproved, but Tawil does not cite a source for this information, and the preponderance of evidence suggests that others were involved in the initial reception.

[249] Muhammad (2012). After the arrival of the al-Qaʿida leadership, the Eastern Shura appears to have taken responsibility for them as indicated in Gopal's interview with Shiekh Muhammad: "We had been under the Nangarhar shura's protection."

Muhammad addresses this question directly by claiming that these three commanders acted without the permission of their parties or the permission of the Eastern Shura when they traveled to Sudan and brought Usama bin Ladin home to Nangarhar in their wake.[250] But given the tight control over the Jalalabad Airport exercised by the shura, it seems unlikely that these three leaders would have been able to leave for Sudan without permission from the governing authorities in Jalalabad.[251] In a conversation with Roy Gutman, Din Muhammad apparently provided a tidy answer for this oddity by pointing out that his brother 'Abd al-Qadir was the leader of one faction within the shura, and it was the other faction led by Engineer Mahmud and Haji Saz Nur that actually invited Bin Ladin.[252]

Some important individuals in charge of the different factions represented in the shura were certainly involved in bringing Bin Ladin to Nangarhar, but it is doubtful that the entire shura was involved in such a plan, since 'Abd al-Qadir is almost never mentioned in connection with al-Qa'ida's movement from Sudan. In fact, it is entirely possible that the three major commanders who left for Sudan in early 1996 were the most powerful figures in Nangarhar who had any prior knowledge of Bin Ladin's impending arrival. Even so, there is some evidence that members of Rabbani's government in Kabul were also aware of the plan to bring the al-Qa'ida leader back to Afghanistan. Wahid Muzhda makes a strong argument against Amrullah Saleh, who allegedly claimed that Bin Ladin came to Afghanistan without the knowledge or consent of Ahmad Shah Massoud.[253]

Although Muzhda admits that he has no firsthand knowledge of such private discussions between Massoud and others, he points out that the presence of 'Abd al-Rab Rasul Sayyaf as a representative of Rabbani's government at the airport in Jalalabad to greet Bin Ladin makes it highly unlikely that the operation to transfer the al-Qa'ida leadership to Nangarhar was conducted without the prior knowledge of the most important elites in Kabul. Even so, it is not yet possible to determine the degree to which the invitation extended to Bin Ladin was originally a Kabul- (i.e., Rabbani-)

---

[250] Muhammad (2007), 202.
[251] The airport is very close to the city of Jalalabad, and it is relatively easy to control access to it. It would have been hard for a plane to take off for Sudan in 1996 if the shura actively wanted it to stay grounded.
[252] Gutman, 90.
[253] Muzhda (2012).

initiated project,[254] and there is evidence that not all of the factions in the Eastern Shura were equally thrilled about the arrival of the al-Qa`ida leadership in Nangarhar. Whatever the case may be for or against the Eastern Shura's complicity in Bin Ladin's flight to Afghanistan, Khalis was not an active member of the shura, and he became visibly involved in this affair only when he invited the al-Qa`ida leader to be his guest at Najm al-Jihad upon arrival.

The History of Najm al-Jihad; Yunus Khalis's Housing Development

When Khalis moved home to Nangarhar from Peshawar in 1994,[255] the governing shura offered him a home in Jalalabad. He rejected their offer and instead built the aforementioned Najm al-Jihad housing development near the southern edge of the city.[256] Najm al-Jihad has evidently gained a reputation in the intelligence community as an al-Qa`ida compound,[257] but the original reason that Khalis built the new development almost certainly had nothing to do with Bin Ladin.[258] Instead, the creation of Najm al-Jihad offers insight into how the aging Hizb leader intended to maintain some degree of political relevance in Nangarhar as he retired and convalesced.

---

[254] It should be stated here that this is exactly what Muzhda suggests. He says clearly that a group of mujahidin leaders who knew Bin Ladin well were sent to Sudan for the celebration of Sudanese independence (presumably in 1996) with the intention of bringing the al-Qa`ida leader back to Afghanistan to assist in crafting a peace settlement with the Taliban. See Muzhda (2012). Muzhda also adds that Bin Ladin's initial response was negative.

[255] Ahmadzai, 46.

[256] Muhammad (2007), 63.

[257] U.S. Department of Defense. "Ali bin 'Attash Detention Documents (ISN 1456; DMO Exhibit 1)." (*New York Times: The Guantanamo Docket.* 2007), 6. http://projects.nytimes.com/guantanamo/detainees/1456-hassan-mohammed-ali-bin-attash. These documents imply that a connection to Najm al-Jihad was admissible evidence used to establish Bin 'Attash's connection to al-Qa`ida, and have this to say about Khalis's housing development: "Nejim al Jihad was an al Qaida housing compound owned by Usama Bin Ladin that is occupied by al Qaida members and their families."

[258] Din Muhammad offers his own assessment of Khalis's reasons for building the new housing development. See Muhammad (2007), 63, 266–267. He claims that it was originally built with humanitarian intentions as a place where widows, orphans and those who were disabled in the war could come to live inexpensively. This may be true, but in Pashtun culture there is a political hierarchy implied in the relationship between host and guest, and it is unnecessarily ingenuous to assume that Khalis was unaware or unconcerned with this relationship of power when he put several thousand people in his debt by creating a neighborhood for them. In any event, when Khalis created Najm al-Jihad, Bin Ladin was no longer in Afghanistan and would not return again for several more years.

Khalis created the Najm al-Jihad housing development on an empty plain immediately south of a former Soviet collective farm.[259] This project was officially named the sixth region (*nahia*) of Jalalabad,[260] but the provision of food and water, the construction of streets and other services were initially arranged by Khalis himself.[261] In fact, Din Muhammad goes out of his way to describe Najm al-Jihad as a humanitarian project. He places the history of the housing development under a section of his book about community service, and he says that Khalis created it for "the families of martyrs and orphans, disabled people and the helpless."[262] Almost as an afterthought, Din Muhammad offers insight into the name of the neighborhood by tying it to the history of the famous jihadi leader known as the Hadda Mullah, whose actual name was Najm al-Din Akhundzada.[263]

Theoretically, Najm al-Jihad was a community built around Khalis's new private home in which people who had lost everything in the recent war could start a new life. The entire Najm al-Jihad project presupposed that Nangarhar was a safer place to live than the rest of the country, and the creation of this new community became part of Khalis's political argument for the alternative to fighting Hekmatyar and others in the civil war. As Hekmatyar assaulted a series of Hizb-e Islami (Khalis) bases in 1995, Yunus Khalis ordered his commanders to surrender their posts and invited them to settle with him in Jalalabad.[264]

---

[259] An official date is never given for the construction of Najm al-Jihad. However, since Khalis lived in the house that he built there and supposedly rejected the Eastern Shura's offer of living in another home, the best guess is that Khalis began construction on the area soon after he returned to Afghanistan in 1994. There is a photograph depicting Khalis sitting in consultation with a group of men on the plain that would become Najm al-Jihad. See Muhammad (2007), 268. The plain is totally empty.

[260] So although Din Muhammad says that Najm al-Jihad was 9 km south of Jalalabad, it is better thought of as part of the city. For the most thorough description of the neighborhood and its creation, see Muhammad (2007), 266–267.

[261] Din Muhammad never explains how long Khalis provided these services, saying only that "at the very beginning" Khalis brought food and water in to Najm al-Jihad at a reduced price for residents. See Muhammad (2007), 266–267.

[262] Muhammad (2007), 266. The title of the section, which begins on page 265, is "Mawlawi Khalis's Community Service During Exile and after Returning Home."

[263] The full explanation is interesting and has clear political overtones that argue for a multicultural vision of Afghanistan: "This town was named Najm al-Jihad because it was the previous location of the great jihadi and spiritual personality Najm al-Din Akhundzada, who in truth was a good witness/evidence of the bringing together of the different tribes of Afghanistan." See Muhammad (2007), 267.

[264] Muhammad (2007), 88–89.

It is impossible to discern Khalis's precise intentions for making this new community. But the creation of Najm al-Jihad had the effect of shifting Khalis's base of support to a new civilian community within Jalalabad at the precise time when his former mujahidin commanders were becoming increasingly independent from him and his ill health was limiting his political activity. Although Najm al-Jihad was the original name of the community, as Din Muhammad notes, it is more commonly referred to as "Khalis Camp or Town."[265] The presence of Khalis Town in Jalalabad has become an enduring reminder of Khalis's ongoing influence on the region. It can be argued that irrespective of the original purpose of this community, there was an association between al-Qa'ida and Najm al-Jihad that can be traced to Bin Ladin's arrival in Jalalabad in 1996. Omar Bin Ladin offers an intriguing suggestion about how this connection may have come about.

According to Bin Ladin's son, a mysterious "Mullah Nourallah," who was then the leader of the province, presented Usama bin Ladin with a large piece of land in Jalalabad, saying, "Build yourself a compound."[266] Various clues suggest that "Mullah Nourallah" was a pseudonym for Haji Saz Nur,[267] further cementing Saz Nur's status as a key al-Qa'ida facilitator in Nangarhar. The location of the plot of land that Nourallah supposedly gave Bin Ladin is unknown, but Najm al-Jihad is the most likely candidate since it is the only named site of a Nangarhari al-Qa'ida compound in the available sources. Abu Jandal describes how the al-Qa'ida "complex" at Najm al-Jihad was

---

[265] Muhammad (2007), 267.

[266] Omar bin Laden, 152.

[267] Omar Bin Ladin claims that Mullah Nourallah was the leader of the province, and Haji Saz Nur fits that name and description better than any other known Nangarhari leader does. Din Muhammad describes Haji Saz Nur as the leader of the Ittihad-e Islami contingent in Nangarhar, and Omar Bin Ladin could easily have taken that to mean that Saz Nur was personally in charge of the entire province. See Muhammad (2007), 202. Omar suggests that Mullah Nourallah was killed in an ambush soon after the Taliban arrived in Jalalabad in September 1996. This matches the known time when Haji Saz Nur (or Mawlawi Saznour) was killed in an ambush along with Engineer Mahmud. See Muhammad (2007), 97–99; Muzhda (2012); and Omar bin Laden, 173, 176. Omar relates that Mullah Nourallah was an old friend of Usama bin Ladin's and that the two had fought together in the 1980s. This is also rumored to be the case with Haji Saz Nur. See Omar bin Laden, 149; and Linschoten and Kuehn, 470. Finally, Omar Bin Ladin's account places Mullah Nourallah at the airport when Usama bin Ladin arrived in Jalalabad, which matches the accounts of Wahid Muzhda and Abu al-Walid al-Masri, who state that Saz Nur was present when the plane landed. See Muzhda (2012); Omar bin Laden, 150; and Linschoten and Kuehn, 135.

converted to a guesthouse when Bin Ladin moved to Kandahar.[268] But even if the al-Qa'ida leader created a permanent presence at Najm al-Jihad that included several buildings,[269] the vast majority of the thousands of residents of the community had little or nothing to do with Bin Ladin's organization.

This distinction between *part* (al-Qa'ida compound) and *whole* (Khalis's residential community) appears to be lost in some accounts; Guantánamo documents released by the U.S. government indicate that at least part of the U.S. intelligence community believes that "Nejim al Jihad [sic] was an al Qaida housing compound owned by Usama Bin Ladin that is occupied by al Qaida members and their families."[270] It is possible that analysts made this assessment based on information that is unavailable to scholars, but on the surface it seems as though the larger history of Najm al-Jihad is simply not well-known in the intelligence community. In the event that the equation of al-Qa'ida's compound at Najm al-Jihad with the entire community is accidental, then it is easy to imagine how any one of thousands of residents of the neighborhood could be construed as an al-Qa'ida operative or facilitator on the basis of this mistaken analytical synecdoche.

The trouble is that although Khalis's neighborhood is no longer commonly referred to as Najm al-Jihad, it is not clear when the Jalalabad community ceased to use that name. If the locals stopped calling the housing development by its original name soon after ground was broken in construction, then perhaps the only part of the area known as Najm al-Jihad in 1996 *was* the al-Qa'ida compound. Unlikely as this may be, only further investigation can uncover the way that this name was actually used in reference to Khalis's town and the al-Qa'ida compound that apparently existed within its boundaries.

No matter what people may call the neighborhood, it would be naive to ignore the political dimensions to the creation of Khalis's new community. However, his housing

---

[268] Abu Jandal (2005).

[269] In his own notes Peter Bergen describes a large al-Qa'ida compound near Hadda outside Jalalabad. By definition, this must be at or near Najm al-Jihad. See Bergen, 172. There is one outlier who describes an al-Qa'ida compound north of Jalalabad, but this does not necessarily mean anything. The writer, 'Abdurrahman Khadr, may be mistaken that the compound was north of Jalalabad or this could simply represent a second al-Qa'ida presence near the city. See Bergen, 173.

[270] U.S. Department of Defense, 6.

development had relatively little in common with the more explicitly radicalized refugee camps in Pakistan that he and other mujahidin leaders had created during the Soviet-Afghan War.[271] Unlike those wastelands of human suffering and political radicalization, Najm al-Jihad and other postwar urban housing developments were intended to be permanent settlements. Khalis, Sayyaf and other Afghan leaders made various attempts to develop periurban property with mixed results.[272] There is no suggestion in any available source that Najm al-Jihad was linked to Afghan mujahidin training camps before the arrival of al-Qa'ida in 1996. In fact, indirect evidence suggests that by 1996 Khalis was no longer the direct commander of a military force.[273] If this is the case, he had less clear need to continue indoctrinating and recruiting new jihadi fighters than other leaders who were still contesting control of large portions of the countryside, such as Gulbuddin Hekmatyar and Ahmad Shah Massoud. Bin Ladin did stay in Yunus Khalis's community at some point in 1996,[274] and he also left a guesthouse there after he moved to Kandahar. However, the al-Qa'ida leader himself did not remain very long at Najm al-Jihad in the summer of 1996 before he travelled southwest to the mountains of Tora Bora.

---

[271] One of the most famous of these is the Shamshatoo Camp of Gulbuddin Hekmatyar. Camps like Shamshatoo were much more than refugee camps. They acted as locations for the indoctrination/education, recruitment and training of fighters for the mujahidin parties. Shamshatoo may still act in this capacity as a site for recruiting young fighters for Hizb-e Islami (Gulbuddin), and has come under scrutiny in both the popular media and the think tank community. See Ron Moreau. "The Jihadi High School." (*The Daily Beast: Newsweek.* 2011 24-April). http://www.thedailybeast.com/newsweek/2011/04/24/the-jihadi-high-school.html; and Omid Marzban. "Shamshatoo Refugee Camp: A Base of Support for Gulbuddin Hekmatyar." (*The Jamestown Foundation.* 2007 24-May). http://www.jamestown.org/single/?no_cache=1&tx_ttnews[tt_news]=4189.

[272] Sayyaf's housing development was built near Paghman. Some of this activity by Afghan elites was doubtless purely speculative and intended to generate revenue as the NATO presence and various NGOs arrived in the Taliban's wake. It is not known to what extent this was also true in the case of Khalis, since the only current evidence is from the biographies and may be biased in his favor. In any event, these materials all cite the building of Najm al-Jihad as a project with specific humanitarian goals.

[273] Admittedly this evidence is mostly indirect. When actual military forces are mentioned in the biographies during this period, they are inevitably commanded by leaders like Engineer Mahmud or Hazrat 'Ali and not by Khalis. For example, see Muhammad (2007), 97. By the end of 1997, Khalis's health would have probably prevented him from participating in any kind of real battle as he had in the 1980s. He was suffering from a variety of illnesses by then, and around 1997 in an accident near his home he injured himself badly enough that he had to be evacuated for treatment to Saudi Arabia. See Muhammad (2007), 111–113.

[274] Linschoten and Kuehn seem to cite al-Masri when they claim that "the Arabs were initially placed in a guesthouse associated with Sayyaf," but it is not clear what this means to us. See Linschoten and Kuehn, 136. Regardless of whether or not his entire group stayed with Sayyaf at some point, Bin Ladin appears to have been "hosted" by Khalis for part of the time they were in Nangarhar.

Omar Bin Ladin was with his father in Jalalabad at this time, and he claims that they moved to Tora Bora within two months of arrival.[275] He attempts to clear the confusion about how they came to occupy the old base by claiming that Mullah Nourallah *gave* Tora Bora to Usama bin Ladin.[276] To be sure, Omar was a child at the time and may have missed some of the details of this transaction, but the value judgment that he transmits about the relative importance of his father's relationship with Mullah Nourallah/Haji Saz Nur is unmistakable. It is known that Haji Saz Nur, Engineer Mahmud and Fazl al-Haq Mujahid were closely involved with bringing al-Qa`ida to Nangarhar. Omar Bin Ladin's account serves to underscore that these relationships, especially with Saz Nur, continued to have far greater practical importance to Bin Ladin after he fled Sudan than his contacts with former party leaders like Yunus Khalis did. This account also reminds us that the al-Qa`ida leader's position became very precarious when Engineer Mahmud and Haji Saz Nur were both killed in an ambush in the fall of 1996 by Haji Shah Wali's forces.[277]

Luckily for Bin Ladin, his worst fears about the Taliban forces that were then arriving in Nangarhar were to prove unfounded. The al-Qa`ida leader's first meeting with the Taliban appears to have taken place at Tora Bora soon after the death of Mullah Nourallah/Haji Saz Nur.[278] The Taliban immediately sought to reassure Bin Ladin that they would protect him. The words of the Taliban representative(s) appear to parallel

---

[275] Omar bin Laden, 175.

[276] Omar bin Laden, 159, 175.

[277] Linschoten and Kuehn point out that the circumstances of this attack are suspicious and poorly understood. See Linschoten and Kuehn, 453. However, Din Muhammad discusses the circumstances of their death in some detail. See Muhammad (2007), 98–100. Engineer Mahmud ignored Khalis's advice to "wait and see" as the Taliban approached Nangarhar, and took charge of the remaining mujahidin/Eastern Shura forces in Jalalabad. According to Din Muhammad, Engineer Mahmud had a relatively positive view of the Taliban and was on his way with Haji Saz Nur to speak with Taliban representatives in Torkham when their vehicle was stopped at a makeshift control point in the road by Haji Shah Wali. Apparently, Haji Shah Wali's forces killed Engineer Mahmud, Haji Saz Nur and many others, but Shah Wali's motivations are unclear. Wahid Muzhda claims that this killing was in revenge for the death of Shemali Khan. See Muzhda (2012). If that account is true, then Shah Wali must be Shemali Khan's brother.

[278] Muhammad 2012; and Omar bin Laden, 175. There is an assertion that the first meeting took place at Yunus Khalis's home. See Linschoten and Kuehn, 138. Linschoten and Kuehn acknowledge the uncertainty on this point, and it is worth nothing that Sheikh Muhammad directly contradicts this argument, stating that "this took place in Tora Bora—not in Khalis' house." See Muhammad (2012).

the content, if not the tone and expressiveness, of Yunus Khalis's much touted remarks to Bin Ladin earlier in the year.[279] This marked the beginning of Bin Ladin's relationship with the Taliban, and at Mullah Omar's invitation he would soon move to Kandahar, leaving only a skeleton al-Qa`ida presence behind in Jalalabad.[280] In spite of Khalis's absence from these accounts of the first meeting between al-Qa`ida and the Taliban, some authors continue to claim that it was Khalis who introduced Usama bin Ladin to Mullah Omar.[281] Those assertions appear to be loosely based on the idea that Khalis was on relatively friendly terms with the Taliban leadership,[282] but the reality of Khalis's interaction with the Taliban was much more complicated.

---

[279] Al-Suri recalls a meeting at which the Taliban spoke very warmly to Usama bin Ladin: "I myself saw a meeting where I was a guest and a visitor of Shaykh Abu 'Abdallah, where several high ranking Taliban entered, among whom was a minister and several officials. The Arabs who were nearby heard them say something to the effect of 'You are the immigrants and we are the followers [of Muhammad].' The minister even said at the end of the meeting: 'We do not say that you are our guests, and we do not say that we are your servants. But we say that we serve the ground upon which you walk.'" See al-Suri, 37. Sheikh Muhammad may be describing the same meeting when he says that "Mawlawi Habibullah welcomed us to Afghanistan and said 'You are safe here and no one will harm you.' This took place in Tora Bora—not in Khalis' house." See Muhammad (2012). In a very similar story, Omar bin Ladin claims that an unnamed Taliban messenger at Tora Bora said "Mullah Muhammad Omar welcomes you and wants you to know that you and your entourage are under the protection of the Taliban." See Omar bin Laden, 175. Abu Musab al-Suri attributes a parallel phrasing when he transmits the statement of protection Khalis made to Bin Ladin: "'I have nothing but myself, and it is very dear to me. However, you are more precious to me, and your well-being is more important than my own. You are our guest, and no one can get to you.'" See Scheuer (2011), 106. For more information on the various paradigms invoked to provide shelter for refugees in this context, see David Edwards. "Marginality and Migration: Cultural Dimensions of the Afghan Refugee Problem." (*International Migration Review* 20, no. 2 (1986)), 313-328.
[280] Abu Jandal (2005). Abu Jandal explains in this interview that after Bin Ladin left for Kandahar, the compound at Najm al-Jihad was converted to a guesthouse to be used occasionally by al-Qa`ida members and their families.
[281] The source for this information in Weaver, and by extension Dressler, et al., appears to be Michael Scheuer. See Weaver (2005); Dressler and Jan, 4; Van Dyk (2006).
[282] "Of the major Afghan party leaders, only Khalis built productive ties to the Taliban; this was, in equal parts, because Khalis, like the Taliban's leaders, is a Pashtun and a religious scholar; he was and is militarily and politically strong in Nangarhar, where the Taliban needed allies to take Jalalabad and Kabul; and because Taliban chief Mullah Omar was a Khalis commander in the jihad." Scheuer (2006), 165.

Yunus Khalis's Relationship with Mullah Omar and the Taliban

Claims about Khalis's relationship with Mullah Omar are frequently discussed as part of a larger argument about Usama bin Ladin,[283] and yet there is no solid evidence linking the three men together organizationally. After the Soviet-Afghan War, Khalis's former commanders took divergent paths. Some of them would become leaders in the Taliban movement, while others such as Jalaluddin Haqqani, 'Abd al-Qadir and Engineer Mahmud became powerful provincial-level leaders. These latter individuals faced a difficult transition in 1995 and 1996 when the Taliban moved north and east out of Kandahar. Some of them, like Jalaluddin Haqqani, decided to work with the Taliban in the hope of maintaining some degree of autonomy.[284] In Nangarhar there was a much more varied reaction to the Taliban's approach.

'Abd al-Qadir left for Pakistan when it became clear that the Taliban would enter his province, but Engineer Mahmud and other former Hizb-e Islami (Khalis) commanders remained and attempted to find a middle path between fighting the Taliban and surrendering the province.[285] By this time, the imperfect systems that were put in place by the Eastern Shura for controlling and preventing violence in Nangarhar were falling apart, and Engineer Mahmud, Haji Saz Nur and many others were killed in the chaotic final days before the Taliban took complete control of the province.[286]

Khalis's position on the Taliban was complex and appears to have wavered between tentative support, disassociation and open criticism. In one conversation in the early days of the Taliban movement, Khalis even congratulated Mullah Omar for his good work.[287] Khalis apparently did not hold this sanguine opinion for very long, and he was able to have a more neutral relationship with the Taliban partly because he was not directly contesting their growing authority as they marched into the east. His former commanders were in an entirely different position, and so Khalis's advice to Engineer

---

[283] For typical examples of this treatment see Weaver (2005); Van Dyk (2006); Lynch, 23; Scheuer (2006), 165; Dressler and Jan (2011).
[284] Muhammad (2007), 86–87.
[285] Ibid., 97–99. Engineer Mahmud ignored Khalis's advice to "wait and see" as the Taliban approached Nangarhar, and took charge of the remaining mujahidin/Eastern Shura forces in Jalalabad.
[286] Ibid., 98–101.
[287] Ibid., 84. At a meeting during Eid in Kandahar, Khalis says to Mullah Omar "You have begun a good project, but don't disarm the mujahidin …"

Mahmud to avoid acting until "the situation becomes clearer"[288] went unheeded. Engineer Mahmud was soon killed, and by the time that the Taliban consolidated their control in Nangarhar, Khalis's view of the movement was already souring.

The vignettes recounted by Din Muhammad depict an increasingly acrimonious and poisonous relationship between Khalis and various Taliban leaders. Din Muhammad recalls several incidents of the Taliban reneging on agreements with Khalis,[289] and he claims that Khalis broadly critiqued the Taliban's heavy-handed enforcement of conservative interpretations of various religious and cultural traditions.[290] True, Din Muhammad is not the best source for unbiased information about the Taliban; his family is well-known for its anti-Taliban politics.[291] And even Din Muhammad notes that Khalis was frequently consulted by the Taliban[292] and that many of Khalis's acquaintances and friends were members of the movement.[293] But these connections and consultations did not guarantee agreement, and Khalis was not a supporter of such Taliban policies as enforcing beard length or interrupting critical agricultural work during the call to prayer.[294] Although details about the nature of Khalis's interactions with Mullah Omar are slim, all of the available evidence indicates that the two men were neither friends nor did they see eye to eye politically.[295]

---

[288] Ibid., 97.

[289] Most significantly, Din Muhammad claims that the Taliban agreed not to attack Nangarhar: "Mawlawi Sahib Khalis from time to time had relations with the Taliban's base in Kandahar. They gave this very same response that 'there isn't a program for Nangarhar, and where there is a program, we will take relations with Mawlawi Khalis.'" This obviously did not work out. See ibid., 96. The year prior, the Taliban had assured Khalis that the weapons depots in Ziruk operated by Mati'ullah Khan's brother Haji Sarfaraz were under no danger of attack. Even as negotiations were ongoing, the Taliban attacked these depots and Sarfaraz lit them on fire before fleeing to Waziristan. See ibid., 87–88.

[290] Muhammad (2007), 104–107. Here Khalis speaks up at a meeting in Kabul after Nabi Muhammadi gave an unsatisfactory response to the Taliban representative. Khalis critiques the enforcement of requirements for beard length and stopping to pray during harvest time when work needs to continue. Brown and Rassler argue that the Haqqani leadership in Loya Paktia expressed similar misgivings, especially with respect to the Taliban's conservative policies regarding women. See Brown and Rassler, 108.

[291] His brothers 'Abd al-Haq and 'Abd al-Qadir were most likely killed by groups affiliated with the Taliban.

[292] There are frequent discussions of Khalis visiting the Taliban leadership and of the Taliban consulting Khalis for advice about various issues. See Muhammad (2007), 84–85, 87, 96, 101, 104–107 and 108-110.

[293] Ibid., 91–92.

[294] Ibid., 104–107.

[295] It is revelatory that we only have evidence of one conversation between Khalis and Mullah Omar in the biographies. The other two times that Khalis attempted to speak with him, Mullah Omar either

In contrast, Khalis was probably on relatively good terms with Usama bin Ladin; Omar Bin Ladin clearly supports this idea in his account of his father's reminiscences with Khalis in 1996,[296] and Talai states that Bin Ladin pronounced Khalis's name with a weighty, reverent tone.[297] But this tells us nothing of the operational and ideological significance of the contact between these two men, and Omar bin Ladin unequivocally states that the most important local facilitator for al-Qa'ida operations in Nangarhar was probably Haji Saz Nur.[298] Khalis contributed significantly to the development of networks of armed resistance in eastern Afghanistan, but the emerging picture of his politics does not support the argument that he was a close ideological or operational supporter of the Taliban or al-Qa'ida. Understanding the development of al-Qa'ida's relationship with eastern Afghanistan requires us to be far more precise about the boundaries and limitations of Usama bin Ladin's connection with Yunus Khalis.

Al-Qa'ida undeniably had an important connection to Nangarhar, but this province was never as important to the organization as Loya Paktia. Some of al-Qa'ida's members fled to Nangarhar from Sudan in 1996, and it seems that they gathered near Jalalabad again as NATO invaded Afghanistan in 2001. However, al-Qa'ida maintained at least three camps operating near Zhawara in Khost throughout the 1990s even after Bin Ladin had left Afghanistan.[299] There is no evidence whatsoever that Usama bin Ladin had a similarly close tie to the camp infrastructure in Nangarhar.[300] Furthermore, Bin Ladin's organization mediated actual operations far more through provincial-level

---

avoided Khalis indirectly by leaving town or snubbed Khalis directly by simply refusing to meet with him. See Ibid., 107, 109–110. This last attempted meeting was especially significant; Khalis was allegedly hoping to speak with Mullah Omar about coming to a peace agreement with the forces of the Northern Alliance. Mullah Omar apparently wanted to have nothing to do with such a conversation and prevented it from even beginning.

[296] Omar bin Laden, 154–155

[297] Talai, 96.

[298] Omar bin Laden, 149–151, 154–156. There is much more material in this book about Mullah Nourallah than Yunus Khalis. The book leaves us with the impression that Bin Ladin met with Yunus Khalis a few times to reminisce, but that this relationship was not necessarily a key one, nor was it operationally significant in any way.

[299] Brown and Rassler, 79. Note that the certain al-Qa'ida sites struck by U.S. cruise missiles in 1998 were in Khost.

[300] In fact, we have relatively little evidence for any continued activities at Tora Bora between 1992 and 1996. For all we know, the base may have been abandoned, or it may have hosted as-yet-unknown groups in this interim period.

commanders like Haji Saz Nur, Jalaluddin Haqqani and Engineer Mahmud than through Yunus Khalis or other mujahidin party leaders.[301] After all, even though Rabbani and other party leaders may have attempted to lure Bin Ladin to Afghanistan before mid-1996 because of a misguided belief in his stupendous wealth,[302] they ultimately failed. This was an age of declining influence for the former mujahidin party leaders, no less so for Yunus Khalis than for the others. Khalis received Bin Ladin warmly as a guest, but it would be a mistake to draw the conclusion that the aging Hizb-e Islami leader was the most meaningful al-Qaʻida ally in Nangarhar Province, much less in Afghanistan as a whole.

Moreover, al-Qaʻida's early development and growth as an organization in Nangarhar seems to have been mostly confined to their participation in the disastrous battle of Jalalabad in 1989.[303] After Bin Ladin returned to Jalalabad in 1996, most of those who followed him from Sudan apparently stayed in Nangarhar for less than a year.[304] Throughout this period, however, al-Qaʻida's training camps in Khost continued their operations. Therefore, Nangarhar's importance to the al-Qaʻida organization is based on little more than Bin Ladin's need for refuge when the Sudanese government ejected him in 1996. This refuge was made possible because of the relative peace of the province during the tumultuous civil war of the 1990s, the absence of the Taliban from the province in the early summer of 1996 and Bin Ladin's strong relationships with an apparently small group of former mujahidin commanders. There is still much to learn about how Nangarhar stayed "open for business"[305] during this period, and there is too little information available about Engineer Mahmud, Haji Saz Nur and Fazl al-Haq Mujahid for us to fully assess the extent of their involvement in al-Qaʻida prior to mid-

---

[301] One partial explanation for Bin Ladin's relatively stronger relationship with these field commanders is that during the 1980s Bin Ladin was most involved at the operational level of the jihad while Yunus Khalis and other party leaders were most concerned with the strategic conduct of the war. Simply because of the level of command where he operated, Usama bin Ladin's mission and planning needs would lead him to develop much stronger connections to other operational commanders like Jalaluddin Haqqani, Haji Saz Nur, Engineer Mahmud, Fazl al-Haq Mujahid and Muʻalem Awal Gul.

[302] Linschoten and Kuehn, 135–136.

[303] Brown and Rassler, 81. Linschoten and Kuehn refer to a telling anecdote about Arabs painting their tents white in a battle near Jalalabad: "The Arabs had marked their tents out in white so that they would stand out. He asked them why. 'We want them to bomb us!' they replied. 'We want to die!'" See Linschoten and Kuehn, 57.

[304] Linschoten and Kuehn, 140.

[305] Semple (2012).

1996. But the evidence assessed for this report cannot support claims that Usama bin Ladin's personal relationship with Yunus Khalis was the essential element in the movement of the al-Qa`ida leadership to Jalalabad from Sudan or in the establishment of a connection between al-Qa`ida and the Taliban.

There is more at stake in the historical adjustment suggested by this analysis than Yunus Khalis's reputation. To be sure, he was a complex figure well known for his avid anti-Shi'a views, and he was much reviled in the West for his marriage to a seventeen-year-old girl in the 1980s when he was over sixty years of age.[306] But irrespective of his controversial religious and gender politics, an investigation of Yunus Khalis as an individual says very little about the development and expansion of al-Qa`ida. Instead, such historical work reveals that Khalis's impact on Afghan politics is measured in his status as a major mid-20th-century Afghan intellectual and a national-level mujahidin commander who helped give rise to both the Haqqani Network and the Eastern Shura. The international community's understanding of the path to peace in Afghanistan today can be significantly enriched by demythologizing al-Qa`ida's connection to certain Afghan leaders such as Khalis. This allows scholars and analysts to more fully engage the complex ideological, political and economic incentives that led men like Yunus Khalis, 'Abd al-Haq, 'Abd al-Qadir and Jalaluddin Haqqani to avoid participation in the Afghan Civil War, and later, to either embrace or reject the involvement of NATO in Afghanistan after 2001.

---

[306] Right or wrong, many Western authors seem obsessed with Khalis's marriage practices. Here are some representative expressions of such prurient interest:

"It was owned by one of Bin Ladin's old sponsors, Younis Khalis, an elderly warlord with a taste for teenage brides." See Wright, 255.

"Their most prominent patron from the anti-Soviet era was Younis Khalis, now an octogenarian who took teenage wives." See Coll, 327.

"He picked up his daughter and kissed her gently on the cheek. I was told he had recently married a 17-year-old girl. I didn't like the fact that he had, essentially, stolen her life. There was nothing decent or noble in this." See Van Dyk (2006).

"Khalis had a well-earned reputation for marrying young women. He took full advantage of Islam's allowance of four wives. In 1990, at age seventy, he married a teenager." See Tomsen, 303. It appears that Tomsen is wrong about the date of this wedding. The actual date may be close to 1983.

Conclusion

As the United States and its NATO allies prepare to withdraw from Afghanistan in 2014, many analysts have begun to uncomfortably discuss the possibility of a return to the Afghan civil war of the 1990s.[307] This necessarily involves a comparison between the current conflict and the final days of the Soviet-Afghan War. But even though appeals to history sometimes offer a welcome insight into today's events, they can also distort the details of past experience beyond recognition when used improperly, leaving us no wiser about what may happen after Kabul's political transition in 2014.[308]

This report has sought to underline the need for dramatically increased precision in our historical analysis of Afghanistan by pointing out the major gaps in our understanding of figures like Yunus Khalis and the specific nature of his connection with Usama bin Ladin and al-Qa`ida. The new sources investigated in this analysis offer a valuable insight into the life and thought of Yunus Khalis, but more important, they suggest an

---

[307] For a representative sample of recent articles that discuss the fear that Afghanistan may slip into a civil war after 2014, see Dexter Filkins. "After America: Will Civil War Hit Afghanistan When the U.S. Leaves?" (*The New Yorker*. 2012 9-July).
http://www.newyorker.com/reporting/2012/07/09/120709fa_fact_filkins; Rob Crilly. "Afghanistan "Facing Civil War When US Troops Leave"." (*The Telegraph*. 2012 14-September).
http://www.telegraph.co.uk/news/worldnews/asia/afghanistan/9543738/Afghanistan-facing-civil-war-when-US-troops-leave.html; Javid Ahmad. "Avoiding Another Afghan Civil War ."
(*www.thedailybeast.com*. 2012 22-October). http://www.thedailybeast.com/articles/2012/10/22/avoiding-another-afghan-civil-war.html; Ryan Evans. "The Once and Future Civil War in Afghanistan." (*The AfPak Channel*. 2012 26-July).
http://afpak.foreignpolicy.com/posts/2012/07/26/the_once_and_future_civil_war_in_afghanistan; and Robert Dreyfuss. "Predictions for Afghan Civil War are Foolhardy." (*The Diplomat*. 2012 18-July).
http://thediplomat.com/2012/07/18/predictions-for-afghan-civil-war-are-foolhardy/.

[308] One of the most common historical generalizations offered by various authors is the idea that all the mujahidin parties fell to fighting among themselves throughout the 1990s. The sources reviewed for this report seem to indicate that this narrative glosses over much of the complexity of the post-Soviet era in Afghan politics. For an example of the blithe appeal to this kind of simplified version of events, see Evans (2012). In his otherwise useful article, Ryan Evans makes a facile characterization of the mujahidin parties' involvement in the civil war: "These [Soviet] troops withdrew in 1989 and the mujahideen parties turned on each other ... marking the third phase." If the currently available sources are to be believed, not all of the mujahidin parties were equally involved in the civil war. This is a critically important distinction because the equation of all mujahidin with the civil war atrocities has consequences for how we deal with different political actors that were members of those groups in the 1990s. A more precise approach might seek to differentiate between the main actors who were most involved in the fight for Kabul.

unexpected connection between the relative peace in Nangarhar during the 1990s and the presence of al-Qa`ida and other militant groups near Jalalabad toward the end of the Afghan Civil War.

The different accounts of the Eastern Shura's role in the fratricidal conflict and Yunus Khalis's involvement in al-Qa`ida's arrival in Nangarhar in 1996 can be misleading if they are read in isolation or out of context. As Frances Brown has recently suggested, the misuse of isolated contemporary anecdotes about the progress of the counterinsurgency campaign in Afghanistan has already had a detrimental effect on U.S. policy implementation.[309] However, the lesson is not that history has no place in improving our comprehension of the current conflict, but rather that precision is necessary in order to make good use of historical comparisons. In fact, if it is applied *accurately*, historical analysis provides one of the best tools for understanding otherwise hidden factors in the spread of political violence.

In the case of Yunus Khalis and Nangarhar, there are two important lessons that deserve increased scrutiny in the future. First, Khalis's rejection of the factional conflict of the early 1990s appears to have been supported both by figures that embrace the Karzai government, such as Haji Din Muhammad, and leaders like Jalaluddin Haqqani and Usama bin Ladin who are almost never thought of for their role as peace negotiators.[310] Ideally, further investigations will elucidate why Haqqani, Khalis and

---

[309] When read together, Brown's recent article "Afghanistan's Need for Reform" and her report for the U.S. Institute of Peace offer a powerful critique of the misuse of locally developed anecdotal insights across the wider Afghan context. As she notes, Afghanistan is complex enough that heavy reliance on anecdotes from one small location (usually a district in her analysis) do not necessarily provide insight into events in other districts. In addition, the heavy focus of government visits on the most successful districts means that far too many of the current anecdotes at a given time will come from the most unrepresentative parts of the country. See Frances Brown. *The U.S. Surge and Afghan Local Governance: Lessons for Transition.* Special Report, (Washington, DC: United States Institute of Peace, 2012); and Frances Brown. "Afghanistan's Need for Reform: We Have Seen the Enemy, and It Is Our Anecdotes." (*The AfPak Channel.* 2012 30-October).
http://afpak.foreignpolicy.com/posts/2012/10/30/afghanistans_need_for_reform_we_have_seen_the_enemy_and_it_is_our_anecdotes.

[310] I stress the "early 1990s" here because after Jalaluddin Haqqani and Usama bin Ladin became aligned with the Taliban in 1995–1996, both would eventually participate in battles against the Northern Alliance. It appears that Khalis was against this latter development, but the only source for this is Din Muhammad. See Muhammad (2007), 109–110 and 112–113. For the contemporary views of the U.S. Department of State on Jalaluddin Haqqani's level of involvement with the Taliban's military efforts in Kabul, see U.S. Department of State. "Afghanistan: Jalaluddin Haqqani's Emergence as a Key Taliban Commander."

other leaders were motivated to end the civil conflict of the early 1990s.[311] Although the U.S. Department of State has apparently indicated that it does not plan to negotiate with Haqqani,[312] officials and scholars who are interested in ongoing efforts to negotiate with the Taliban can still benefit from an understanding of why Haqqani and certain other leaders chose to halt major military operations soon after Najibullah's Soviet-backed government fell in 1992. Second, and somewhat more surprisingly, the fact that the Eastern Shura was able to maintain a relative degree of peace in Nangarhar during the civil war never prevented al-Qa`ida and other groups from operating there.[313]

Various sources attest that Yunus Khalis, Jalaluddin Haqqani and Usama bin Ladin actively attempted to prevent the spread of the violence in the Afghan Civil War in the early 1990s,[314] but clearly this was not a manifestation of general pacifism on their part. The fact that so many of Yunus Khalis's commanders and associates rejected the fight for Kabul after 1992 indicates that they may have had dramatically different political goals than more familiar figures from the civil war such as Gulbuddin Hekmatyar, Ahmad Shah Massoud and Burhanuddin Rabbani. It is critical to understand why the different desired outcomes for these figures led some of them to destroy Kabul and others to focus on consolidating their control over their home provinces. By unraveling Yunus Khalis's political views and his effect on the politics of the Eastern Shura, we can approach the question of how different regional actors react to the potential of intra-

---

(*George Washington University: The National Security Archive.* 1997 January). http://www.gwu.edu/~nsarchiv/NSAEBB/NSAEBB295/doc05.pdf.

[311] Brown and Rassler argue that Haqqani's actions during this period are reflective of his version of an autonomy-seeking, upland Pashtun approach to politics. See Brown and Rassler, 84, 105, 108. Future historical and political work would profit from a study of Jamil al-Rahman's efforts to create an independent Salafi state in Kunar and other autonomy-seeking political movements in upland eastern Afghanistan to see if there are meaningful similarities between the movements in Loya Paktia, Kunar, Nangarhar, and elsewhere.

[312] The Haqqani Network was officially named a "foreign terrorist organization" on 7 September 2012, which significantly increases the legal difficulty for any future U.S. administration attempting to enter a negotiated peace settlement with the organization.

[313] The economic incentive to keep trade through Jalalabad and the Khyber Pass open meant only that the Eastern Shura needed to generally keep the road open and the airport safe for traffic. There was no incentive for the shura to chase down groups that were plotting terrorist activities elsewhere as long as they kept relatively quiet and did not disrupt economic activities within Nangarhar.

[314] For information on Haqqani's and Usama bin Ladin's involvement as negotiators and mediators, see Brown and Rassler (2012). For information on Khalis's role as a mediator, see Muhammad (2007), 88–90; Scheuer (2011), 105; and Omar bin Laden, 154.

Afghan war with greater precision.[315] However, this renewed interest in the history of the Eastern Shura is frought with a variety of other difficulties.

The Eastern Shura was a multilateral body that negotiated Nangarhar's transition out of the Soviet-Afghan War and into the era of the Taliban. According to the known sources, which are admittedly likely biased in favor of the shura, this organization elected to pursue a path that kept the worst of the Afghan Civil War's violence out of Nangarhar.[316] This alone should be impressive enough to encourage scholars of Afghanistan and civil war conflicts to learn more about the shura and other similar institutions in other parts of eastern Afghanistan. However, eastern Afghanistan is a difficult place to administer even in the best of circumstances, and it should not surprise us that the Eastern Shura was limited in its ability to actually "govern" Nangarhar. There was relatively little institutional or physical infrastructure undamaged by the previous wars,[317] and although the area around Jalalabad was more peaceful than Kabul at the time, the shura was not necessarily interested in actively preventing foreign jihadi organizations from taking root on its soil.

Al-Qaʿida took advantage of the combination of relative peace and light governance to build a short-lived presence in Nangarhar in 1996, and they may not have been alone as they did so. If the ambush against the four UN officials in 1993 is any indication, there may have been an extremist presence in the province throughout the 1990s.[318] This must serve as a warning to anyone who remains under the illusion that achieving a reasonable level of security in Afghanistan is sufficient to prevent the return of al-Qaʿida or other terrorist organizations to the more lightly governed districts of the outlying provinces. Ultimately, we have only begun to scratch the surface of Yunus Khalis's considerable historical interest, and the revelations from these new primary sources represent only a fraction of the material that is still undiscovered. If the

---

[315] Antonio Giustozzi has already done a good job of delving into the details of the civil war and warlords in western and northern Afghanistan. See Antonio Giustozzi. *Empires of Mud: Wars and Warlords in Afghanistan.* (New York : Columbia University Press), 2009.

[316] The clearest statement of how Haji Din Muhammad and Yunus Khalis understood the role of the Eastern Shura can be seen at Muhammad (2007), 88–90.

[317] Even as late as 1996 as the Taliban approached Nangarhar, the factions in Kabul were making bombing runs on buildings in Jalalabad, including what is presumably now the governor's palace (*kala*). See Muhammad (2007), 101.

[318] For a brief report on the ambush, see U.S. Department of State (1994).

materials discussed so far are any indication, a renewed interest in Khalis, the Eastern Shura and other neglected Afghan political figures will likely lead to surprising and fruitful discoveries about the negotiation of radical politics and civil conflict by leaders in the critically important region of eastern Afghanistan.

Biographical Appendix:

Khalis Family Members or Hizb-e Islami (Khalis) Affiliated

'Abd al-Haq: 'Abd al-Haq was 'Abd al-Qadir and Haji Din Muhammad's brother and a major commander in Hizb-e Islami (Khalis). 'Abd al-Haq mostly operated in and around Kabul, and like many other commanders in Khalis's party, he apparently withdrew from the fight for Kabul before the struggle led to civil war. He was killed in late 2001 after he entered Afghanistan with a small group to build an anti-Taliban movement from among the local people.

'Abd al-Qadir: Little is known about 'Abd al-Qadir's conduct during the Soviet-Afghan War, but he was connected with Hizb-e Islami (Khalis). He is also a brother to 'Abd al-Haq and Haji Din Muhammad. After the end of the war, 'Abd al-Qadir became a major leader in the Eastern Shura based in Jalalabad. He fled the city when the Taliban took Nangarhar Province in 1996. He was killed soon after he was installed as the governor of Nangarhar by the Karzai government.

Anwar al-Haq Mujahid: Yunus Khalis's eldest surviving son. Anwar al-Haq was a leader in the "Tora Bora Front" for several years until his 2009 arrest in Pakistan took him out of operation. He was released from prison in Pakistan in late 2012 with a group of other important Taliban prisoners as part of a Pakistani effort to restart peace talks with the group.

Engineer Mahmud: Mahmud was one of the most important Nangarhar-based commanders in Hizb-e Islami (Khalis) and a member of the Eastern Shura during the 1990s. Engineer Mahmud was relatively close to Usama bin Ladin, and traveled with Haji Saz Nur and Fazl al-Haq Mujahid to speak with the al-Qa`ida leader in Sudan in early 1996. As a result of this embassy, the al-Qa`ida leadership chose to come to Jalalabad after being exiled from Sudan. Engineer Mahmud was killed in late 1996 along with Haji Saz Nur.

Haji Din Muhammad: Haji Din Muhammad was the deputy chief of Hizb-e Islami (Khalis) during the Soviet-Afghan War. His family is staunchly anti-Taliban, and he wrote a biography of Yunus Khalis that is one of the more important primary sources for this study. He was the governor of Nangarhar and then Kabul Province after the fall of the Taliban in 2001.

Mawlawi Jalaluddin Haqqani: One of the most important commanders in Hizb-e Islami (Khalis) during the Soviet-Afghan War. Haqqani was central to both the evolution of Khalis's mujahidin party and, later, the movement that became al-Qaʿida. He is the founder of the Haqqani network, and is often referred to in eastern Afghanistan as *"Haqqani Kabarri"* (Haqqani the Scrapman) because of his involvement in selling scrap-metal after the end of the Soviet conflict. He took the nickname (*takhalus*) "Haqqani" after he graduated from the Dar al-'Ulum Haqqaniyya in Akora Khattak near Peshawar, Pakistan.

Mati'ullah Khan Wali Khel: Although he is not well known today, Mat'iullah Khan was one of the most important commanders in Hizb-e Islami (Khalis). He was based out of the Ziruk base in modern day Paktika, and was one of the founding commanders of the Hizb-e Islami (Khalis) party.

Mawlawi Muhammad Nasim: Muhammad Nasim was Yunus Khalis's eldest son. He was arrested for speaking out against the government soon after Daoud Khan's 1973 coup. Muhammad Nasim was killed while in the custody of the Kabul government around 1978.

Muhammad Yunus Khalis: Yunus Khalis was educated in pre-Partition India, including lessons he took from the founder of the Dar al-'Ulum Haqqaniyya, 'Abd al-Haq Haqqani. Khalis held a variety of jobs in journalism, education, and other fields, and he became involved with the anti-leftist Islamic opposition to the Kabul government in the 1960s. He would eventually become the leader of the Hizb-e Islami (Khalis) mujahidin political party. His commanders included Jalaluddin Haqqani, 'Abd al-Haq, Mati'ullah Khan, and Engineer Mahmud. Khalis was neutral during the Afghan Civil War, and in 1996 he hosted Usama bin Ladin for a brief time in Jalalabad. Tora Bora was Khalis's principal base in Nangarhar Province.

Other Mujahidin Party Leaders/Commanders

'Abd al-Rab Rasul Sayyaf: Sayyaf was a professor at the Faculty of Islamic Law at Kabul University when the nascent mujahidin movement began to take shape under Professor Ghulam Niazi in the late 1960s. Sayyaf is a gifted Arabic speaker and used his linguistic skill to great effect on fundraising trips to Saudi Arabia during the 1980s. He became the leader of a party known as "the Islamic Union" (Ittihad-e Islami), and is still a major political figure in Afghanistan.

Ahmad Shah Massoud: Massoud was a Panjsheri mujahidin commander for Jami'at-e Islami. He became a great enemy of Gulbuddin Hekmatyar and the power struggle between these two after 1992 contributed greatly to the destruction of the Afghan Civil War. Massoud was killed on 9 September 2001 during an attack which appears to have been executed at the instigation of al-Qa'ida.

Burhanuddin Rabbani: Rabbani was a lecturer at the Faculty of Religious Law at Kabul University and became involved with Professor Ghulam Niazi's political group in the 1960s. He eventually became the leader of the Sunni mujahidin political party that included the highest percentage of non-Pashtun members: "the Islamic Society" (Jami'at-e Islami). Rabbani had a large number of Tajik and Uzbek commanders, including the famous Ahmad Shah Massoud.

Fazl al-Haq Mujahid: A major Nangarhar-based commander of Hizb-e Islami (Gulbuddin) and a member of the Eastern Shura during the 1990s. He traveled with Engineer Mahmud and Haji Saz Nur to speak with Usama bin Ladin in Sudan in 1996.

Gulbuddin Hekmatyar: Hekmatyar was a student when Niazi's political discussion groups at Kabul University began to take on structure in the 1960s. Hekmatyar became active in the student circles connected to these Kabul Islamist discussion groups, and rose in the ranks of the Muslim Youth organization (Zawanan-e Musulman). He eventually went on to lead the Hizb-e Islami (Gulbuddin) political party. He became an implacable foe of Ahmad Shah Massoud, and their struggle for supremacy with several other mujahidin leaders after 1992 was one of the major causes of the destruction of the

Afghan Civil War. Hekmatyar is a prolific author and has written dozens of books in Pashto on diverse topics in politics, religion, grammar, and history.

Haji Saz Nur: Haji Saz Nur was a major commander for Ittihad-e Islami in Nangarhar and a member of the Eastern Shura in the 1990s. Saz Nur was relatively close to Bin Ladin and figures prominently in several primary sources for the help that he gave the al-Qaʿida leader in 1996. He traveled with Engineer Mahmud and Fazl al-Haq Mujahid to speak with Usama bin Ladin in Sudan in 1996.

Mawlawi Jamil al-Rahman: Jamil al-Rahman was an important mujahidin leader from Kunar Province. He studied at the Panj Pir Madrasa in Pakistan, which had a strong Salafi orientation. Sources differ in their accounts of Jamil al-Rahman's alignment during the Soviet-Afghan War, but he appears to have been affiliated with either Yunus Khalis or Gulbuddin Hekmatyar. Around 1984 he apparently broke with all of the mujahidin factions, and returned home to Kunar. Later he would found a Salafi party called the "the Society of Invitation to the Sunnah and the Qur'an" (Jama'at al-Da'wa ila al-Sunna wal-Qur'an), which contested control of Kunar with several different mujahidin factions. These groups eventually held elections, and in 1991 Jama'at al-Da'wa declared the creation of an independent state of Kunar. Jamil al-Rahman was assassinated that same year.

Mawlawi Nasrullah Mansur: Nasrullah Mansur was a mujahidin leader from Zurmat District of Paktia Province. He was one of several influential eastern clerics who took part in a series of abortive attempts in the late 1970s to find a leader who could unite the various mujahidin factions. He became a commander in the Harakat-e Islami party and was a fierce enemy of the Hizb-e Islami (Gulbuddin) party. Although Nasrullah Mansur is now dead, the group he founded, known as the Mansur network, is still actively fighting against the government in Afghanistan.

Minhajuddin Gahiz: A writer and political activist who founded an obscure group known as the Hizb al-Tawabin together with Yunus Khalis and several other leaders. Gahiz also founded an Islamic political publication under his own name ("gahiz" means "dawn" in Pashto). Many of the eventual leaders of the seven Sunni mujahidin political parties published articles in *Gahiz*. Gahiz was killed in 1972.

Muhammad Nabi Muhammadi: Nabi Muhammadi was a graduate of the Dar al-'Ulum Haqqaniyya. Nabi Muhammadi was chosen as a compromise leader to unite the squabbling mujahidin factions in the late 1970s with the creation of the Harakat-e Inqilab-e Islami. This unity party failed in its original purpose, but Nabi Muhammadi continued on as the leader of Harakat throughout the war.

Professor Ghulam Niazi: Niazi left Afghanistan to be educated at al-Azhar in Egypt, where he was exposed to the ideas of the Muslim Brotherhood (Ikhwan al-Muslimin). He began holding political discussion group meetings in the 1960s, which later evolved into some of the first anti-leftist mujahidin political movements in Afghanistan. Both Gulbuddin Hekmatyar and Burhanuddin Rabbani looked to Niazi as a political and spiritual leader.

Sayyid Ahmed Gailani: Gailani was the leader of one of the largest networks of Sufis in Afghanistan at the start of the Soviet-Afghan War. He used this network to help create "the National Front" (Mahaz-e Milli), one of the two Sufi mujahidin political parties.

Sibghatullah Mujaddidi: Mujaddidi was the leader of one of the largest and most politically influential Sufi networks in Afghanistan during the 1960s and 1970s. He eventually founded "the National Salvation Front" (Jebha-ye Nejat-e Milli). This was one of the two Sufi mujahidin political parties.

Al-Qa`ida Affiliated Individuals or Relatives of Usama bin Ladin

Abu Musab al-Suri: Al-Suri (whose real name is Mustafa bin 'Abd al-Qadir Setmariam Nasar) was a strategist and trainer with ties to al-Qa`ida. He wrote about some of his experiences with Usama bin Ladin, and gives a brief account of a meeting between Yunus Khalis and the al-Qa`ida leader in 1996. After spending several years in detention in a number of countries following 9/11, he is rumored to have been released from Syrian custody during the 2011 to 2012 timeframe.

Ayman al-Zawahiri: The former head of Egyptian Islamic Jihad and a key al-Qa`ida member and propagandist, al-Zawahiri has served as the leader of the latter group since the death of Usama bin Ladin in Abbottabad, Pakistan. While not much is known about al-Zawahiri's relationship with Yunus Khalis, al-Zawahiri provides a very brief description of the assistance that Khalis gave to Usama bin Ladin in 1996.

Nasir al-Bahri: Al-Bahri (also known by his kunya Abu Jandal) played multiple roles for al-Qa'ida and served for a period during the 1990s as Osama bin Ladin's bodyguard. He provides insight into how the al-Qa'ida "complex" at Najm al-Jihad was converted to a guesthouse when Bin Ladin moved to Kandahar.

Omar bin Ladin: A son of Usama bin Ladin, Omar provides a first-hand account of some of his father's relationships with Afghan commanders in Nangarhar and the time his father spent in both Nangarhar and Tora Bora.

www.ingramcontent.com/pod-product-compliance
Lightning Source LLC
Chambersburg PA
CBHW080431290526
45791CB00008BA/2457